"We need to talk"

Tough Conversations with Your

Spouse

From Money to Infidelity
Tackle Any Topic with Sensitivity and Smarts.

PAUL COLEMAN, PSY.D.

adamsmedia
Avon, Massachusetts

For George and Fran Coleman,
Angels that you are;
You were magnificent.

Published by
Adams Media, an F+W Media Company
57 Littlefield Street, Avon, MA 02322. U.S.A.
www.adamsmedia.com

ISBN 10: 1-59869-879-6
ISBN 13: 978-1-59869-879-4

Printed in the United States of America.

J I H G F E D C B A

Library of Congress Cataloging-in-Publication Data
is available from the publisher.

This publication is designed to provide accurate and authoritative
information with regard to the subject matter covered. It is sold with
the understanding that the publisher is not engaged in rendering legal,
accounting, or other professional advice. If legal advice or other expert
assistance is required, the services of a competent professional person
should be sought.

> —From a *Declaration of Principles* jointly adopted
> by a Committee of the American Bar Association
> and a Committee of Publishers and Associations

Many of the designations used by manufacturers and sellers to distin-
guish their product are claimed as trademarks. Where those designations appear in this book and Adams Media was aware of a trademark
claim, the designations have been printed with initial capital letters.

This book is available at quantity discounts for bulk purchases.
For information, please call 1-800-289-0963.

Contents

Acknowledgments

ONCE AGAIN I'M eternally grateful to Mike and Pat Snell of the Michael Snell Literary Agency. This marks our tenth book and twenty years together. I simply wouldn't have had my writing success without you. Every author should be so fortunate.

My thanks to Chelsea King at Adams Media for the great book concept, for bringing me on board, and for sensational editing. And thanks to Casey Ebert and the designers at Adams Media for all their help on the production side of things.

Thanks to my wife Jody and our children—Luke, Anna, and Julia—who are always supportive and understanding when I'm preoccupied with writing.

And to Sam. Thirteen years was too short. But what great memories. . . .

Now on to the next project. . . .

Introduction

Navigating Smoothly In Rough Conversational Waters

SOMETIMES THE MOST important topics a married couple discusses are also the most delicate. How do you steer through a thorny issue where the wrong word can lead to hurt feelings or a deep emotional rift? How do you tell the person you love something he or she might not want to hear? What do you do when your partner gets defensive? This book is designed to help you navigate choppy conversational waters with two essential skills: consideration and know-how. It will provide you with indispensable scripts and power phrases to move you and your mate quickly past the various tricky spots couples encounter when discussing touchy subjects, while offering a treasure trove of cutting-edge tips and tools.

The words and phrases I suggest are not the only words you should use, but they are a great place to start. If you study the tone of the sentences and phrases I prescribe, you will soon get a feel for what works, and you'll be able to use your own words to achieve the same successful end. Some of you may be thinking, "It's not just a matter of saying the right words but saying the right words with the right attitude." You're absolutely correct. Anyone can say to a spouse after a disagreement, "Fine, I'll do it your way." But if that line is spoken with sarcasm, the words won't solve a thing. That's where this book is unique. It teaches you how to de-escalate a disagreement so that your partner's viewpoint becomes possible for you to understand. And as you aim for understanding—genuine understanding—your attitude will shift from hurtful to helpful.

The first two chapters reveal the most essential, easy-to-remember communication tools that even someone who doesn't like reading self-help books can learn and apply in no time at all. (And if your spouse is one of those people, ask him or her to just read those two chapters. If applied with sincerity, the suggestions will work.) Chapter 2 also discusses the SAIL approach to communication, a simple, four-step method that is easy to remember and use. When all else fails, if your conversations are going nowhere but downhill fast, the SAIL method will instantly put you and your mate back on track—sometimes in a minute or less!

Each of the remaining chapters describes one (or more) of the common scenarios many couples face that can easily stir up trouble if not handled properly. The issues lurking beneath those topics are discussed and many suggestions are offered to move those conversations along with tact to a successful conclusion. At the end of each chapter is a sample script designed to show you how the opening minutes of an effective conversation might go. The scripts purposely show occasional communication errors because even the most effective communicators mess up. The scripts also show you how to quickly recover from those mistakes and get back on track—which is also what successful communicators do.

It's simple. If you communicate effectively with your spouse, most of your problems will fade into the background and you can get on with the business of living a happy, satisfied married life.

Chapter One

Five Hidden Conversational Traps

PHIL HUGGED HIS wife Connie. She flinched.

"Why do you push me away like that?" Phil asked.

"I'm just trying to sort through Emma's school papers."

"Yeah, right," Phil said, walking away.

Connie sighed loudly. "And maybe I don't like being pawed at all the time."

"I wasn't pawing," Phil said.

"And if I hadn't moved away you'd have tried to do more and you know it. Why can't you just be affectionate without it always turning into something sexual?" she asked. "Oh, just forget about it."

Phil didn't know whether to pursue the conversation or drop it. He hated moments like that.

Do you and your spouse ever have conversations like that? I call those interactions "Clash, Rehash, and Dash" and the pattern goes something like this:

Spouse #1: "Why don't you . . . Why can't you . . . You never . . . You always. . . ." (A blaming response; rehashing old issues.)

1

Spouse #2: "Well I would except that you always. . . ." (A defensive response followed by a blaming response.)

Spouse #1: "No, no that's not true; you always exaggerate. . . ." (More defensiveness, more blaming, and no real effort to understand or get to a helpful resolution.)

Spouse #2: "I don't know why I bother talking. You never admit it when you're wrong." (More blaming, perhaps walking away from the conversation.)

Any couple can have a conversation like that but successful couples have them infrequently. When they do occur, successful couples stop those conversations from escalating. If you recognize yourself somewhere in that pattern, then you're reading the right book. Help is on the way—and making conversations with your spouse go from tough to tender is easier than you imagine.

The Culprit Behind Most Conversational Goof-Ups

The key reason couples find it hard to tackle certain topics is anxiety. Couples are usually anxious for at least one of the following reasons:

- They don't know what to say or how best to say it.
- They worry about starting an argument or debate.
- They worry about being blamed or hurting feelings.
- The discussion usually goes off-track and becomes frustrating.
- They don't know how to calm an overheated conversation.

It's a vicious cycle. Heightened anxiety impairs the conversation skills you do possess, and impaired communication skills—

especially during touchy conversations—intensifies anxiety. The result? As you spin your wheels and become more nervous or agitated, the goal of achieving meaningful conversations with your spouse seems further out of reach.

Anxiety also disrupts your sensitivity. (See the quiz, What Is Your Sensitivity Quotient, in this chapter.) Your sensitivity level is similar to your home smoke alarm. If the alarm is too sensitive it will go off when you have candles burning. If it is not sensitive enough it may not go off until a fire has started raging.

If you have too much anxiety during conversations you will be oversensitive to your partner (and undersensitive to your own needs) or undersensitive to your partner (and oversensitive to your needs). People who react with oversensitivity to a partner's needs tend to lose their confidence and give in to demands just to keep the peace. People who react with undersensitivity to a partner's needs will overwhelm their spouse, see little merit in what the spouse is saying, and feel entitled to get their way.

What Is Your Sensitivity Quotient?
Answer "Rarely True," "Sometimes True," or "Often True":
1. I feel inadequate, stupid, or wrong in difficult conversations.
2. My partner often turns my complaints back around on me and I lose my confidence.
3. It's easier to give in than to argue.
4. I feel guilty when I get my way.
5. It's mostly my fault when conversations go wrong.
6. I hate compromising when I know I'm right.
7. I get loud during conversations, otherwise my spouse won't listen.
8. I don't like being told what to do.

9. If I feel strongly then my spouse should see it my way.
10. If we disagree, one of us must be wrong.

> *Scoring:* You are undersensitive to your own needs the more you answered "Often True" to statements 1–5. You are undersensitive to your partner's needs the more you answered "Often True" for statements 6–10.

This book teaches two essential tactics: how to manage anxiety during conversations so your level of sensitivity is neither high nor low; and how to find the right words to allow a conversation to come to a rewarding conclusion. If you aren't anxious but cannot find the right words, the conversation may never get going. If you know the right words but are too anxious, the conversation will implode soon after it gets underway.

What Your Senses Can Tell You

It's not only about verbal language; it's also about body language. During a conversation you don't just use your ears to understand the words; you use many of your senses—including your intuition—to understand the meaning behind the words. In any conversation, the listener instinctively pays attention to the nonverbal signals much more than the verbal. When there is a disconnect between what someone says and what they really mean, the listener gets mixed signals and confusion takes over. Here is how an effective conversation looks, sounds, and feels.

What Your Eyes Show You

Imagine you are watching a video of a couple successfully engaging in a touchy conversation. Assume they don't always agree;

that each can be a tad stubborn or argumentative at times during the dialogue, and the topic is an important one (so it raises their anxiety). Since this couple possesses conversational skills, mutual goodwill, and can keep their anxiety levels in a manageable range, what do you think you would see if you turned off the volume and just watched them? Physically, they would be positioned in a way that conveyed openness and a desire to listen. No arms defensively crossed, no eyes rolling. There'd be no finger pointing or dismissive hand gestures. They'd be making eye contact and perhaps touching one another occasionally. There would be no dramatic or hostile body language—no hitting walls or throwing objects and no physically threatening behavior. Impatient at times, they'd nonetheless hear each other out rather than loudly interject in the middle of each other's comments. Facial expressions would show concern or mild aggravation or perhaps understanding—maybe a smile or two—but never contempt or disdain.

What Your Ears Tell You

Now turn off the picture and listen only to the sound of their conversation. It wouldn't be boring or monotonous. If they got loud and angry the anger would rise but soon fall back to a more moderate level. They would interrupt each other occasionally. However, the interruptions would not be disruptive to the flow of the conversation. Interruptions would be viewed as a sign of interest, not rudeness. There'd be no name-calling. There might be a few "you" statements (blaming remarks), but each would be able to quickly admit when they were wrong or disrespectful. They'd each aim to understand the other as much as they aimed to be understood. They would ask questions to gain understanding, not to place each other on the witness stand. If the topic was a particularly emotional one, neither would take it too personally if the other said something out of line. They would accept that when the topic is very upsetting, unkind or provocative words are often spoken that are not really meant. Overall, the conversation would have a beginning ("We need to talk about this"), a middle ("Let's examine it more closely"), and an end ("Let's take these steps to address our concerns").

What It "Feels" Like

Imagine you and your spouse are taking a nature walk, but are not allowed to speak. Where you walk is unexplored by you and has many places of interest—flower beds, creeks, rocky hills, a waterfall, a fenced-in area with animals, hilltops where you can see for miles. How would this feel to you as you tried to maneuver toward the places you wanted to investigate? If you and your spouse are competitive and argumentative, or if one of you is more controlling, you would feel pushed or pulled in every direction, either not going where you'd like or engaging in a tug-of-war to get your way. You would start to feel tense, angry, and impatient. If you are a couple that communicates effectively, there would be no pulling or pushing. There may be a gentle tugging to move in one direction but there would also be a willingness on both your parts to take turns leading and following without struggle. You wouldn't feel rushed. You'd know there was time to linger over some areas if you wish, even if your partner was less interested. It would feel light, easy, warm, and loving.

Using those descriptions as a guide, how do your conversations rate? What would observers notice if they watched you and your spouse having a conversation about a touchy subject? What changes could you make during your next conversation?

The Five Toxic Traps

Open up almost any self-help book on communication and you're likely to be advised to not interrupt when your partner is speaking. Well guess what: Happy couples interrupt each other even more than unhappy couples do and it isn't a problem. Your interpretation is what makes the difference. Unhappy couples view an interruption as rude. Happy couples interpret it as a sign of interest. Or maybe you've heard the age-old advice "never go to bed angry"—but couples who are successful communicators understand that sometimes a person needs to withdraw temporarily to sort through feelings and thoughts and that waiting another day to resolve an issue is sometimes wise, especially if one tends to be volatile.

You've also read that avoiding conflict only leads to a buildup of resentment and ultimately an explosion. Seems logical, but according to researcher John Gottman at the University of Washington, if both partners are conflict-avoiders by nature, and if the couple experiences at least five times as many positive interactions as negative, they can stay happily married for the rest of their lives even if they rarely argue. So toss aside some of the old surefire advice and pay close attention to these five toxic troublemakers. They are:

- Rough start-ups
- Possessing a black-and-white mentality
- Believing all relationship problems can be resolved
- Confusing feelings with facts
- Allowing arguments to escalate

If you can eliminate any of these, your ability to communicate effectively—with sensitivity and smarts—will improve as quickly as you can say "We need to talk. . . ."

Rough Start-Ups

The first minute of a discussion is the start-up. If the start-up begins with a harsh tone or a hasty accusation, it is more likely that the conversation will end in failure. Failed conversations make it more likely that future conversations will either be avoided, will end prematurely, or will lead to escalating arguments and no-win debates. In fact, if a discussion that starts up heated does not calm down to a milder, more respectful conversation within the first three minutes, odds are it will fail. Couples have a small window of opportunity to open conversations with respect and consideration—and stay there.

Women are more likely to detect relationship problems before men see them, are more likely to complain about those problems, and are therefore more likely to begin touchy conversations with a sharp-edged tone. Men are more likely to withdraw or shut down once a conversation gets tense or when they feel disrespected or not listened to. The man's shutting down will frustrate the woman and make it more likely she will open future conversations with more fire and grit, thereby setting off another round of the argue-withdraw pattern.

Examples of Emotionally Charged Phrases to Avoid
- "You always. . . . You never. . . ."
- "You don't know what you're talking about."
- "Are you bringing that up *again*?"
- "Are you going to act the way you did the last time we tried to talk?"
- "I don't know why I even bother talking to you."
- Any name-calling and swearing.

Examples of Negative Labels

- "You're just like your mother."
- "You're lazy . . . selfish . . . inconsiderate . . . controlling."
- "You have no clue how to be a responsible parent."
- "You never take responsibility for yourself."
- "You don't care at all how I feel."

Open conversations with goodwill by simply stating what you'd like to talk about, give behavioral examples of what you like and dislike, don't judge or blame, ask for feedback, and come up with ideas on what can improve the situation.

A Black-and-White Mentality

"You should have done this. You shouldn't have done that. A spouse should always. . . ." A "should" mentality is an inflexible insistence that one person's way of thinking is necessarily the right way or the best way or the only way. This mentality closes off discussion. If you possess a "should" mentality you are not really interested in understanding your spouse's view but in converting your spouse to your view. This leads to stubborn standoffs and tugs of war.

Many issues that couples disagree about reflect personality and background differences—or even personal preferences. What time should the curfew be for a fifteen-year-old? What's the best way to discipline a defiant child? How much time should a couple spend doing things together? How often should they make love? What percent of their income should they save?

There are no right or wrong answers to these questions. Those are examples of the many gray areas in life where couples must negotiate, not pontificate.

Conversation Peace

A black-and-white mentality will soon come across as an "I know best" mentality. That's how parents speak to children and superiors speak to inferiors. Once your marital relationship has a parent–child feel to it, neither of you will be happy. Inevitably, the spouse who feels in the one-down position will try to balance the scales of power directly (by being stubborn and argumentative) or indirectly (getting even in subtler ways such as losing one's desire for sex, "forgetting" important things, overspending, and so forth). Relationships must feel fair to flourish.

Part of the difficulty in letting go of certain black-and-white thinking patterns is it means letting go of our ego. We identify who we are with the beliefs we hold, but many of our beliefs are simply habits. If you grew up believing it was never okay for one parent to go on a vacation or relaxing trip without a spouse, you will argue with your spouse when he or she wants to attend a three day work-related conference on some exotic beach. If you grew up having very little money and no extras, you may either want to spend money more freely now or may want to save as much as possible to ensure that you will never be poor again. Regardless, if your spouse takes a different approach to spending and saving, there will be conflict.

Let's consider an example. Kate and Mike wanted to buy a new car. She didn't care what kind it was as long as it was comfortable for the entire family and that they bought it quickly, as a summer trip was upcoming. Mike was methodical and weighed the pros and cons of a dozen car models. His slowness annoyed Kate. Mike was annoyed because Kate "should" be more concerned about car quality and price range. To Kate, Mike "should" ease up and not be so rigid about making decisions. That debate will never get them anywhere.

How might they handle that difference? Three steps:

1. Stop trying to insist that the other's approach is wrong.
2. Ask the question "What would you like me to understand that you don't think I do understand?"

   Mike might answer it this way: "I'd like you to understand that I take my responsibility to this family seriously, and I don't want to make a major purchase we might later regret."

   Kate might answer this way: "I'd like you to understand that it is frustrating when you take so long to make up your mind about things and that I'd like us to have a new car before we leave for our vacation."
3. List what they'd be willing to do (not what they'd *like* to do) that would meet each of their concerns to some extent.

So Mike might agree to be methodical but limit his search for a car to a handful of car models and stick to a deadline. Or Kate might help him with his search.

Once a couple bypasses the "should" mentality, a world of possibilities opens up for them.

All Problems Can Be Solved

We live in an age where we can instantly find answers for most anything. So when a couple engages in yet another "here we go again" argument, each spouse believes the other must be stubborn or selfish since all problems should be solved with the right amount of compromise and teamwork.

That simply isn't true. Yes, some problems can be permanently fixed by a simple solution like with Pete and Jen. Pete and Jen often forgot to make their car payment which was due on the tenth of each month. They finally decided to have the funds automatically withdrawn from their checking account. Problem solved. However, most of the issues we face in life cannot be solved once and for all; they can only be managed. These include—but are not limited to—problems involving:

- Health
- Child-rearing
- Money
- Personality differences
- Differences in values

Don't despair. You are already accustomed to managing—not solving once and for all—certain daily problems. For example, if you commute to work and traffic is often heavy, you've probably learned to live with the fact that on some days there will be traffic delays. If you are raising children, you're probably overtired and have much less free time for yourself or your spouse. You can make changes here or there but the problem—less time to do things you'd like to do—can only be managed, not resolved.

Awareness Is Key
For many couples, the awareness that some problems have no permanent solution is an eye-opener. They realize they've been

banging their heads trying to eliminate some thorny issue only to have it reappear later on. They discover that trying to solve certain problems is itself a major problem. Once they learn to let go of their demand to be rid of certain difficulties and find a way to learn to live with them, their "problem" no longer seems so problematic.

How do you best manage a recurrent relationship problem? You must be willing to talk about the issue periodically, not to solve it or debate it, but to inquire, "How should we handle it *this* time?" (Because there will absolutely be a *next* time.) Then you agree on a course of action that will move you forward that day without resentment. Sometimes you'll get your way, sometimes you won't.

Do You Confuse Feelings with Facts?

I hear conversations like this every day in my office:

> Spouse 1: "You ignored me at the barbecue."
> Spouse 2: "No, I didn't. You were by my side most of the time."
> Spouse 1: "I certainly *felt* ignored. My feelings aren't wrong, they just *are*."

This conversation is already a landmine waiting to be stepped on. Many people confuse their feelings with facts. If I *feel* ignored, I *was* ignored. If I *feel* offended, I *was* offended. Judging another person is not a feeling—it's an opinion. "I feel that you care more about your job than you do about me" is an opinion. "I feel lonely when you work so much" is a more accurate expression of one's emotional state. Feelings are important data but they are not always accurate reflections of reality. Feelings are preceded (often subconsciously) by a line of reasoning that may be faulty—thereby creating a more distorted feeling. For example, in one day I had two separate couples attend counseling and each spoke about their anger over a recent office holiday party. For the first couple, the husband was angry that he spent most of the time alone in a corner. He expected his wife to introduce him to everyone and stay by his side. For the second couple, the husband was angry that his wife stood by him the entire party. He felt "mothered." Each husband felt angry, but the feelings were highly subjective and based on their own line of reasoning as to what should happen when a couple attends a party together.

Once people regard their feelings as facts, they then insist their feelings be validated. By validation they usually mean "honor my feelings as true." Again, the feelings may *feel* true for the individual but are not an accurate representation of what happened in the situation.

The Power of Feelings

During a touchy conversation you don't have to admit guilt when you aren't guilty. "I can see that you're upset that I stood by your side at the party. But it wasn't my intention to 'mother' you. I just assumed you'd feel more at ease since you didn't know many people. Next time I'll give you more space. All right?"

Feelings are best used not as weapons but as clues to underlying assumptions. (Usually, those assumptions are based on the "should" mentality I've already discussed.) Then examine those assumptions and see just how reasonable they are.

Allowing Arguments to Escalate

Many couples view an escalation of an argument as natural. They don't realize how imperative it is to put escalating arguments into reverse. It's there for everyone to see and yet it is overlooked as a major reason for conversation breakdowns. If couples avoided this trap, their ability to communicate effectively would skyrocket. Think of an effective conversation as a game of catch where the ball is tossed back and forth at a fairly regular rate of speed. An occasional fastball is okay but you want to avoid the situation where a fast toss is followed by an even faster toss and so forth until all precision is lost.

Effective communicators don't always keep their cool, but their emotional ramp-ups are quickly followed by a calming down so the conversation never gets out of hand.

How to De-escalate a Conversation Quickly

When you're involved in an escalating conversation, you'll know it. At least one of you will be more accusatory, more hostile, less gentle, and less willing to listen. As soon as you notice the conversation is escalating you *must* try to de-escalate it. Your spouse must be willing to cooperate, not stubbornly insistent on staying argumentative. Two ways to put an escalating conflict into reverse:

1. Point out something your spouse said that has merit.
2. Point out something you said that was wrong, inflammatory, or hurtful.

Imagine an argument about money has escalated and you say one of the following:

- "You're right. We do need to save more."
- "I agree. I do sometimes buy things without shopping for a better price."
- "I'm sorry, I shouldn't have said that. What I meant to say was. . . ."

- "It was wrong of me to call you cheap. I know you're just trying to help us manage our money better."

It's almost guaranteed that the tone will automatically improve and the two of you will have a more effective conversation. Of course, you may have to de-escalate many times during a particularly difficult conversation but that's okay. Touchy conversations are inevitable and are supposed to be a bit bumpy.

Your Next Step

Now that you are aware of the key conversational blunders you want to avoid, there is one more thing to do. You need to understand how the conversations you have every day with yourself can help or hinder communication. That's what the next chapter is all about.

Chapter Two

The SAIL Approach
to Conversation

WORDS ARE POWERFUL. Saying the right words in the right way can soften hard feelings, settle conflicts, and strengthen bonds. That's usually all it takes for the average married couple to feel pretty good about their relationship.

The better a couple knows one another, the more they might communicate using subtext. The subtext of a discussion is what's not stated directly and must be figured out by the listener. If the couple is happy and secure, chances are the subtext is easy to figure out and creates no conflict. For example, sometimes a hug really means "let's have sex." If the couple is happy they may or may not have sex, but the meaning will be understood and the outcome won't cause problems. If one or both partners are angry or anxious, they may say things that sound pleasant and relaxed ("How about a movie tonight?"), but underneath they worry "Why doesn't he want to spend time with me?" When the subtext isn't clear, people don't say what they really mean so conversations get confusing very quickly.

How you use subtext in your conversation has to do with your personality and your experiences in life. To get to the bottom of what's bothering you in your marriage and what makes some of your conversations go haywire, first look at yourself. A lot of the short-circuiting that happens when conversations get confusing is due to lack of personal insight, not just lack of conversation skill.

Why You Do the Things You Do

Let's say your husband wants sex more often than you do (it's a stretch, I know). Imagine also that you like to have sex when the timing is just right—no kids nearby, no fatigue, not busy with other matters. But he's like a firefighter—armed and ready on a moment's notice no matter what the conditions. Imagine further that your husband likes sex to be mildly adventurous (in the shower, the hot tub, a "quickie" while the kids are still awake, and so on) whereas you prefer something less risky.

Now the question: Why do you each *persist* in your unique attitudes?

1. *It represents a difference of personality and taste, nothing more.* If so, those differences must be accepted rather than fought over, and compromises must be reached occasionally.

2. *The personality difference has widened and become exaggerated due to repeated arguments and debates.* If so, you must take responsibility for how your words or actions have worsened the problem and change some of your ways. (For example, the more one person demands sex, the more the other may refuse, causing the first to be more impatient and demanding, causing the second to be even less interested in having sex.)

3. *There are background experiences that have caused hurt or anxiety, which contributed to your current attitude.* You might have

to re-examine long past issues and see if they are in fact getting in your way now. (Sometimes a conversation is "touchy" because it is literally touching on some old issue you'd rather not revisit.)

Any conversation can get off-track simply because one of you is having a bad day. However, if you have many tense conversations, or if conversations are avoided in order to steer clear of an argument, you can bet that factors from categories two and three mentioned above are operating. Unless you try to delve a little deeper into what makes you tick—and reading this chapter will help tremendously—the phrase "we need to talk" will be about as welcoming as a dentist's drill.

Three Questions to Help You Understand Yourself

Learning what makes you tick is a lifelong process. If you answer the following three questions with just a little thought and honesty, you will understand more clearly what your emotional strengths and weaknesses are and what you need to do to make immediate improvement. Ready?

What Is Your Preferred Approach to Feeling Happy?

I began thinking about this after reading the scholarly book *Healing the Culture* by Robert Spitzer. He discussed four levels of happiness that, for purposes here, I will condense to three:

1. Seeking immediate gratification
2. Seeking ego gratification through achievement or winning
3. Finding something good beyond yourself

Interestingly, these are levels that children go through as they age. An infant cares only about getting needs met immediately. He doesn't care who it inconveniences. As the child matures, he gains satisfaction by achieving goals—learning to walk and talk, read and write, ride a bike, and so on. Eventually, it is hoped that all children realize that there is a greater good beyond having their own needs met. Sharing or sacrificing for others becomes important and doing good becomes an end in itself.

We all operate at the immediate gratification level once in a while (Level One). We're hungry and all we care about is eating a meal. Or we're tired and we just want to relax. Or we purchase something on a whim. We all operate at the ego level occasionally as well (Level Two). We feel happy when we win the award, get the promotion, make more money, or achieve something we are proud of. Hopefully, we've all made sacrifices for others and realize that something greater than ourselves exists (Level Three). While we can operate using all three levels, we tend to emphasize one of those levels as our preferred way of feeling happy. That is what will drive us the most.

LEVELS OF HAPPINESS IN YOUR MARRIAGE

In a marriage, if you are usually at Level One, selfishness and inconsiderateness will take precedence. At Level Two, couples compete and debate. For one to be right, the other must be wrong. For one to get, the other must give—or not get. At Level Three, couples see value in doing good for the relationship even if it means sacrificing something for themselves. In fact, no sacrifice is that bad because a greater good is getting met.

If your conversations with your spouse are routinely problematic, one or both of you is operating primarily at Level One or Two.

Searching for the right words won't put an end to ineffective communication if the words you are looking for are meant to manipulate the other to get what you want or to "win" the argument. To rise above this, keep in mind that it's normal to operate at the lower levels of happiness—we all do it every day—but the highest level must also be achieved regularly if the relationship is to be satisfying and fulfilling.

What Did You Not Get Growing Up?

In the classic book, *Getting the Love You Want,* author Harville Hendrix asks readers to think about what they didn't get emotionally from their childhood but wish they had. When I ask people that question, I hear the following common answers:

- "**I wish** my mother or father was around more."
- "**I wish** I didn't have so many burdens."
- "**I wish** I didn't feel so alone."
- "**I wish** there was more affection and warmth."
- "**I wish** I wasn't forced to do things I didn't want to do."
- "**I wish** home life was more secure."

The answer to the question *"What did you not get growing up?"* often reveals something that continues to be unresolved currently in a person's life. For example, if a young girl had to always look after her siblings growing up while her parents were away much of the time working, then she might now be a person who puts her needs aside for others and wonders "When will it be my turn?" Consequently, she may feel taken for granted in her marriage. A man who had a strained relationship with his dad growing up and who learned to handle the worries of a childhood without asking for help will often dislike being told what to do. He will probably be an unskilled communicator since discussing feelings was simply not the family's way growing up. He'll try to solve problems on his own, and *maybe* he'll talk about it later. Someone who craved affection growing up may always feel the affection she receives now from a spouse isn't enough—or she may be uncomfortable expressing and receiving affection.

When you discover what it was you wish was different growing up, you will probably see how that same issue is operating now in your marriage.

How Did You Cope Growing Up?

There are basically five ways we cope with adversity. The five F's are: fight, flee, freeze, fold, and face matters head-on. Think back on a time as a child where you were scared or hurt. Which of those five coping styles was your primary method? A *fighter* might be persevering but aggressive. Someone who avoids conflict might *flee* or hide in their room. Someone who *froze* was unable to think clearly or make decisions. Someone who *folded* meekly surrendered to the situation and didn't try to change it. Someone who *faced* problems head-on learned confidence.

So How Do You Cope Now?

How do you cope (manage your anxiety) when your conversations get sticky? When you know you will face an argument if you try to raise a certain topic? Do you get aggressive? Withdraw? Try to talk but can't get the words out clearly because your mind has frozen? Give in to what your partner wants? Or do you try to hang in there and find better ways to communicate?

Conversation Peace

The late Dr. David Viscott discussed a quick method for understanding your emotions in his book *The Language of Feelings*. Emotional pain in the here-and-now is felt as hurt or loss. Anger is resentment over having been hurt or at having lost something valuable. Guilt is usually the anxiety you feel about being angry. Depression is the inability to manage hurt, anger, and guilt. Anxiety is the fear of future hurt or loss. So, if you are depressed, first look at what you feel guilty about. If you feel guilty, look at what makes you angry. If you feel angry, what is the hurt behind your anger?

If you aren't facing the issues squarely and with respect, chances are you will blame your spouse for the manner in which you handle conversations instead of realizing that you are using a worn-out coping style. If you are aggressive, you'll blame your spouse for being inconsiderate or hurtful. If you withdraw, you'll say your spouse is too harsh and that forces you to flee from conversations. If you freeze up, you'll say your spouse is too clever with words and you can't think clearly when he or she talks to you. If you submit, you will feel depressed, ineffective, and overwhelmed and accuse your spouse of being controlling.

Your choice now can be to face the situation directly, with improved communication skills, some courage, and some greater insight into why you tend to act the way you do during difficult conversations.

The SAIL Method

When conversations about touchy subjects are successful, you are doing four things right. The following four items form the mnemonic SAIL:

1. **State** straightforwardly what's on your mind. No detours, no attacks, no judgments.
2. **Accept**, don't emotionally oppose, your spouse's thoughts and feelings. You don't have to agree with your partner, but you must accept that for now your spouse does think and feel the way he or she does.
3. **Inquire** as to the real **importance** of the issue at hand. What's at stake for you emotionally?
4. **List** creative ideas to resolve or address mutual concerns.

Let's examine these more closely and see why they are essential.

State (Don't Berate)

Make comments that are straightforward, to the point, and without a tone that says "Guilty as charged!" Don't expect to be unemotional or to completely avoid saying things you shouldn't— everyone has a hard time during certain conversations. Try to be mindful when your voice is getting louder, your tone more judgmental, or your words more unfriendly. This is where the need for gentle start-ups and the ability to de-escalate an argument (discussed in Chapter 1) come in handy. Also be aware when you are saying very little or nothing at all and therefore giving the message "Can we stop now?" Minimal involvement in a conversation can be just as disruptive (and aggressive) as harsh tones and unfair accusations.

Accept the Reality of the Moment

Acceptance happens when you don't emotionally oppose the reality of what is happening. Acceptance is not passivity. (If you're getting rained on, acceptance doesn't mean you won't reach for an umbrella. It means you won't be agitated about it in the process.) If you get agitated, you are really saying "This shouldn't be happening!" when it *is* happening. Imagine your spouse being difficult—demanding, argumentative, unwilling to hear your view. Acceptance means giving up the inner battle to oppose what has already occurred. It is better to say to yourself "I accept that my wife is really upset and not listening to me right now" than to say "This is unacceptable!" If you emotionally accept the reality of the moment, you still can make efforts to change it, but you will abandon the agitation that usually accompanies a desire to get a spouse to be different. When you accept the moment as it is, you can be patient. If you can accept the idea that you and your mate will disagree, that feelings of love may take a backseat to annoyance, that a spouse will act in ways you don't always agree with, you can more quickly get to the "What are we willing to do about this?" stage instead of lingering at the anger and blaming stage. When you accept that your mate is very emotional or unreasonable, you will listen better. You stop listening when your inner mind-chatter is busy judging your spouse. Your being a better listener will probably help calm your spouse down. Spouting something like "How can you say that!" (nonacceptance) will make your spouse defensive.

If you don't like what your spouse is saying, it's okay to say "Please lower your voice," or "I don't agree with your version," or "If you continue to call me names I'm walking away from this discussion." However, if you cannot emotionally accept that at the moment your spouse is talking to you with certain attitudes, opinions, and word choices, you will probably start a debate, escalate the conversation into an argument, or reflexively shut down.

Acceptance is vital because neither you nor your spouse will be a perfect communicator all the time.

During difficult conversational moments, repeat the phrase "I don't like this but I accept it." It will help you remain calmer and less reactive.

Inquire about the Importance

What is really at stake in the conversation? What propels this issue forward for you? What would deeply trouble you if the issue were not resolved? Look inward and tap into the deeper issues that lie at the foundation of the thorny topic at hand. Usually these deeper issues involve one or more of four underlying themes:

- Lovability (Am I lovable? Cared about?)
- Safety (Do I feel safe? Are my children safe? Do I feel secure in this relationship?)
- Self-esteem (Am I good enough? Competent? Worthwhile? Attractive? Desirable?)
- Fairness (Am I being controlled? Bullied? Taken advantage of?)

According to research conducted at the University of Washington, at least 70 percent of touchy conversations are not about the topic at hand but are a stand-in for a deeper concern. So, arguing about who takes the dog out may really be a statement about a lot of perceived unfairness. Arguing about money and spending may be tapping into an issue about control or security. If deeper issues are lurking but are not brought out into the open, any surface conversation you have will be useless.

Many times the hidden issue did not originate in the marriage but in a past relationship or during childhood. When you have a marital issue, ask yourself "When did I feel this way in my childhood? In prior relationships?" If the origin of the problem is from your background, you may be expecting your spouse to fix an issue that he or she didn't create. Clues that hidden issues exist:

- Frequent overreactions or misunderstandings
- Believing you can read your spouse's mind and accusing him or her of malicious intentions
- Arguing over small things
- Using extremely harsh words; making biting comments; conveying disgust
- A subtle awareness that your unhappiness is not just due to your marital situation

If you feel convinced that the topic at hand is the only issue that is being triggered, you may be correct. If the conversation gets bogged down, ask yourself, "If there is an underlying issue, what might it be?"

List Creative Ideas to Deal with the Issue

One reason conversations get stuck in the mud is the tendency for couples to affix blame and to debate "facts" rather than simply see if an agreed-upon solution (although perhaps only a temporary solution) is possible. For example, a couple once came into my office and immediately began arguing about an upcoming birthday party they were hosting. He knew his wife disliked his sister and immediately defended his sister while accusing his wife of putting him in an impossible situation of having to choose between his sister and his wife at family gatherings. His wife became hostile and defensive and repeated stories of how she had been disrespected by various members of his family over the years.

I finally asked this question: "What would you each like to see happen at the upcoming birthday party?" He answered that he wanted his sister to be invited and he glared at his wife, daring her to disagree. His wife said she had absolutely no problem with that. He was stunned. His wife then said that she wanted him to say nice things about her in front of his family. He said he had no problem with that. His wife was stunned. In about thirty seconds the entire issue was softened and made much more manageable simply because the couple looked for solutions rather than problems.

During difficult conversations it's usually necessary to discuss the problem where all facets of the issue can be addressed. But once a debate starts or one of you feels like quitting the conversation, try to think about a temporary solution that would ease the situation. Don't focus on what you want, but rather on what you are willing to do to make the issue less inflammatory.

The Sticky Issues Ahead

I hope you understand now that with the right words, an awareness of common roadblocks to avoid, and a dollop of sensitivity, any conversation with your spouse can feel like holding hands—maybe a little too tightly at times—but not so bad, either.

The remainder of this book will describe in more detail how to have a useful conversation about a variety of common but sticky issues most couples usually face. Feel free to begin anywhere.

"We need
to talk"

Chapter Three

Manipulation and
Game-Playing

P EOPLE ARE OFTEN afraid to say what they mean so they must
resort to "playing games" in order to bring about a desired goal.
We've all done it. But it obstructs clear and considerate communication and therefore shaves away feelings of intimacy. Your goal is
to recognize the ways you manipulate or control your partner and
develop more straightforward methods of relating.

Games Couples Play

"Manipulative" isn't always a bad word. Ever try to playfully coax
someone to accompany you somewhere when you knew he or she
would rather not go? That's being manipulative but hardly in the
category of "nasty" or "controlling." The key difference is this: Do
you care at all about the other person's feelings and desires or do
you care only about yourself? You might manipulate someone in
a friendly but pushy way, and yet back off when it's clear to you
the other person doesn't appreciate what you're doing. When being
manipulative is entirely self-serving or you make the other person
pay a price for not doing what you want, you've crossed a line.

Here are three scenarios:

1. **Linda and Bob** are married nine years and have three kids. They had a very brief discussion one night about whether the kids were old enough to enjoy a vacation at Disney World. Would the cost of the vacation be worth it if the children were too young to fully appreciate the trip? Three days later Linda had finished two books on Disney World and what to do there with kids aged three to seven. She looked into the cost of airline and hotel reservations and what the best deals were. Bob wasn't even sure he wanted to go to Florida but Linda showered him with all this new information. "Please can we go?" she said. "Pretty please?" She made him smile. He told her he'd been thinking about the idea but hadn't made up his mind. She agreed it would be a financial sacrifice for them but also figured out ways they could save money in other areas. Bob chuckled at her intensive planning and agreed to book the trip.

2. **Bill and Amy** are married five years. Some of the novelty has worn off in their relationship. They both work, and they have one child with another on the way. He joined a softball league and looks forward to every game. Amy finds softball a bit boring but does her best to sit in the stands and cheer him on. Lately she has skipped some games and is standoffish when he comes home. She tells him she dislikes that he has several beers after each game because alcohol makes him grumpy. She complains that he rarely wants to go out with just her but yet he makes time for his buddies. Bill knows Amy has a point but he resents it when she pouts and acts demanding. He sometimes doesn't tell her about a softball

practice or double-header until the last minute—otherwise he'd be hearing her complain for days.

3. **Hal and Stacey** have been married two years. Hal had stood Stacey up on what was supposed to be their first date. He called her three days later with a vague explanation about his impossible job and begged for a second chance. He did show up this time—but almost three hours late without a phone call. However, to make up for his thoughtlessness he had picked her up in a limousine he had hired for the night and they "did the town." Stacey wanted to be furious at him and tell him to never call her again, but she didn't. After all, "What kind of guy goes to all that trouble for a first date? Shouldn't you cut him some slack?" After a year of dating (sometimes on schedule, sometimes not) Hal and Stacey got married. But Stacey sometimes wonders if she made a mistake.

All three of those scenarios involve at least one person trying to manipulate the other. But the manipulations are qualitatively different from one another and are good indicators of how happy the relationship is. In the first scenario, Linda and Bob are the happiest of these couples. Yes, Linda acted a tad childish with her "pretty please" comment but it was an obvious ploy that came off as "cute" precisely because it was not her usual way of relating. Linda was clearly very excited about a possible trip to Disney World but was willing to delay the trip if their budget didn't allow it. Her manipulation was mild, transparent, and fun and Bob found it easy to go along with Linda's wish.

In the second scenario, Bill would withhold information about his softball games because he didn't want to hear Amy complain. Amy complained about his time spent away from her by pouting and being distant. Bill and Amy had a modestly happy relationship but it needed work. Their method of trying to manipulate each other added to their sense of ill-will. Neither enjoyed the other's manipulations and actually resented them. But the quality of their manipulative tactics—however off-putting—was something that could be changed for the better with effort.

Hal and Stacey have a very destructive relationship. In fact, Hal is a highly controlling and verbally abusive husband. His gimmick with the limousine was just a way to deflect criticism from him. If Stacey were to ever complain about his thoughtlessness, he could always point out the generous things he does for her. Controlling people must always win a debate and they always try to get the other person to doubt themselves. In two years of marriage she has second-guessed herself many times which is one reason she is so miserable now.

Understanding a Manipulative Person

The more manipulative and controlling people are, the less healthy their relationships will be. Still, it is the rare individual who doesn't manipulate a spouse at times. The person who attends an event with his spouse that he'd rather not attend and has an "attitude" is being manipulative. The husband who hates confrontations and instead sleeps in the spare bedroom to convey that he's angry about *something* is being manipulative. So is the wife who proclaims "If you really loved me you would. . . ." A manipulation is a clear indication that the individual or the marriage—or both—can't stand up to the scrutiny of truth. It is a sign that honesty and straightforwardness won't get you what you want. It indicates a degree of immaturity in the relationship—the greater the use of manipulation or power tactics, the greater degree of immaturity.

Where Does Lying Come Into It?

Lying is a form of manipulation. When the evidence against you is strong and you continue to lie, you are hoping to persuade the other person that his or her perceptions are distorted, wrong, or even paranoid. (That becomes a form of emotional abuse.) There are fundamentally two motivations to manipulate a spouse:

1. To get what you want and at the same time avoid rejection or conflict
2. To dominate and control (usually found in people who are verbally and possibly physically abusive)

This chapter will focus primarily on the first type of motivation. The second motivation is too important a topic to be limited to just a few pages. Besides, people who are abusive and highly controlling are not open to having a constructive dialogue—which is what this book is all about.

Why Couples Get in Trouble

Manipulativeness isn't fatal. However, it can impede intimacy, add to resentments, and weaken the relationship. Many couples are already stressed—crazy work hours, kids with busy after-school schedules, high mortgage payments—and can't afford the additional strain that occurs when partners manipulate one another.

Bear in mind that manipulation occurs when more direct communication is somehow regarded as ineffective or threatening. Good people who are nevertheless prone to using manipulation include:

- People pleasers
- Rejection-sensitive individuals

- Conflict-avoiders
- Those who have secrets they hope their mate won't discover
- Those with chronic (and often vague) physical complaints
- Rescuers (those who bail others out or put aside their needs to save someone from their poor judgments)
- Victims (can either be very needy or are fed-up rescuers who feel unappreciated and taken for granted)

People who fall into one or more of those categories think: "How can I get what I want without offending anyone, being rejected, or losing something important? How can I get others to like me?" They can express anger but they usually require a large build-up of resentment before they feel entitled to express it. Then they feel guilty or worried afterward.

Talking to Yourself and Reprogramming Your Brain

If you recognize yourself in any of the above categories, the first and most important conversation you must have is with yourself. Byron Katie's wonderful book, *Loving What Is*, offers a useful and simple method of helping people change their irrational beliefs. Her first suggestion is to ask yourself "Is this really true?" It's a terrific place to begin. For example, if you are a people pleaser, ask yourself "Is it *really true* that if I say 'no' to someone, they will stop liking me?" Or, "Is it *really true* that I must always manipulate my partner to avoid conflict or to get what I want?" Our brain operates with one primary goal: to help us survive. Any time you feel anxiety about something (such as talking to your spouse) your brain regards the source of anxiety as a threat to you. It wants you to eliminate the threat. If you lower your anxiety by running from

Talk Alert

If you are in a controlling/abusive relationship, trying to get the abuser to listen to reason will fail. Looking for ways to "understand" and feel sorry for the abuser will result in you becoming more stuck in the relationship and unable to trust your own judgment as time passes. Look for these signs (not all will apply) that you are in an abusive/controlling relationship:

- He began the relationship being overly generous. You were his "one and only" very quickly.
- She subtly criticizes your appearance, your style of dress, your family, your hobbies or interests, and makes you feel that when you do ordinary things (for instance, having lunch with friends or spending time and money on a hobby) you are being selfish, distant, unloving, or insensitive toward her.
- He is possessive. He calls you on your cell phone a lot or asks for details about your day because he's really checking up on you.
- It soon becomes all about her—what she wants and needs.
- He demeans you, makes you feel foolish, criticizes your decisions.
- She can be terrifying when angry and makes others reluctant to confront her for fear of her wrath.

If you wish to learn more about this type of relationship, read *The Verbally Abusive Relationship* by Patricia Evans.

or manipulating the situation, you will repeat those same behaviors the next time you feel threatened. If you try to stop being manipulative and face the situation squarely, you will temporarily experience a sharp increase in anxiety. That's your brain's way of getting you to revert to your old pattern. If you hang in there and succeed in having a more direct, constructive conversation with your spouse (despite moments where it doesn't go well) your brain will discover that what was once threatening (fear of rejection or conflict) is now much less so.

Your brain will then make it easier for you to carry out more effective conversations in the future. If you try to stop manipulating and start being more direct, you will initially become more anxious—the conversations will be awkward or difficult—and you

Conversation Peace

Are you rejection-sensitive? People whose needs were not met consistently as children or who—for whatever reason—have low self-esteem can develop a heightened sensitivity to feeling rejected. They take things very personally. Their partners may lie or hide the truth about an innocent event because they know it will be misinterpreted. Rejection-sensitive people can become quite controlling ("If you loved me you would . . .") and require reassurances they are loved. If this is you, begin to look for alternative explanations for a partner's behavior that paints him in a more favorable light ("He didn't return my call because he was busy, not because he doesn't care about me").

will want to revert to your former methods. If you persevere, your conversations will be more successful and less threatening and your need to manipulate will diminish.

Good Openings

If you feel you are being manipulated or not being told the full story about something, you have a right to be angry or annoyed. However, if your spouse is a bit manipulative due to fear of conflict or rejection, your anger can fuel this anxiety. Your goal is to confront your spouse about being manipulated in a firm, clear, but nonthreatening manner.

- "Every time you act that way I lose faith in our ability to simply talk things over. Can you please say what's really on your mind?"
- "Last night you were angry and you gave me the cold shoulder instead of talking things out. You can be angry if you need to be, but I need you to be more open."
- "Please tell me why you have a hard time being direct and straightforward. I promise I'll listen and not argue."
- "Let's make a deal. We each say what's bothering us and we try to figure out a way to work things out without twisting each other's arm. Okay?"

If you tend to use manipulation to avoid conflict or to get your way, becoming more straightforward means you may have to experience some degree of conflict and you may *not* get your way. (If you succeed at getting your way most of the time then either your spouse is very flexible and easygoing or you are more manipulative than you should be.) It can be helpful to state your new goals to your spouse so you can both be on the same page.

- "I usually avoid discussing our credit card bills because we'll just argue about spending. I don't want to do that anymore. I'd like us to meet each other halfway and come up with a spending plan we can both live with."
- "When I'm annoyed with you I like to go out with my friends and leave you home because I know it will make you mad. I don't want to do that anymore, but I need your cooperation so we can find a way to talk things out constructively."
- "I sometimes make up excuses to avoid having sex because you won't take no for an answer. I don't like playing games like that. Can we find a way to not turn sex into a battle of wills?"

Good Follow-Throughs

As anxiety rises or the conversation gets a bit testy or off-track, the tendency will be to use manipulation to force your will on the other or to run from the conversation and use manipulation later to get even or get what you wanted in the first place. The goal of the follow-through phases is really anxiety management. It's all about staying calm, optimistic, and fair-minded instead of agitated, scared, or self-serving. If anxiety rises, don't fight it or push it away. Simply say to yourself, "I accept that I'm anxious . . . I accept this isn't always easy . . . I accept that I want to be more open in my conversations." Acceptance helps you stay in the moment without being distracted by anxiety.

- "Ordinarily I'd shut down from this conversation about now but I won't this time. Bear with me."
- "It feels like you're trying to make me feel guilty. Let's agree not to do that kind of thing."
- "It's not about getting what I want; it's about both of us being fair."

- "This is the hardest part of a conversation for me; when you get mad and defensive and I feel like walking out. Let's stay on track."
- "You hate it when I don't always tell you the whole story and I hate it when I tell you things and you get argumentative. We have to find a way to make openness and honesty a safe thing to do."

As you can see, while the topic is about manipulation, the real issue is about keeping conversations safe and meaningful so manipulation doesn't have to happen in the first place.

Not-So-Good Openings and Follow-Throughs

When a good person manipulates a spouse, he or she does so with the firm belief that the spouse would somehow be uncooperative if a more direct approach were taken. While that may be true, it works both ways. Sometimes it is difficult to talk to your spouse precisely because they feel they have been toyed with, manipulated, or treated unfairly.

Blaming a spouse misses the point: If your relationship is to rise above manipulations, it must start with a willingness to put aside game-playing no matter what the cost.

- "You're so childish when you do that." (Name-calling rarely helps.)
- "Are you going to force me to go to your office party, which I hate?" (Better: "It's okay if you go to the party but I always have a miserable time. Would it be okay if I didn't go?")
- "I do these things I shouldn't because my self-esteem is low." (Hoping your spouse will feel sorry for you is a manipulation.)
- "If you wouldn't _____, then I wouldn't _____." (Don't assign blame.)

- "I manipulate things because I have a hard time trusting. I've been betrayed by others in the past." (Hard luck stories give you a ready-made excuse to remain manipulative.)
- "I only manipulate you like that when I feel scared or worried about what you might say." (That may be true but it cannot be used as an excuse anymore.)

If you want your relationship to contain fewer instances of manipulation, you must take a no-nonsense approach to the problem. Your goal is to have more honest, open, and fair conversations so there simply is less of a need to manipulate.

Sample Script

"We need to talk"

Phil and Toni are in a marriage that isn't all that bad but could be much better. They're each tired and overworked and feel a bit underappreciated. There is no one area of conflict or concern that really stands out but they feel an uneasy undercurrent to almost everything. Good days are good, but the "off" days make them crazy. Toni realizes that her favorite way of manipulating her spouse is to play the victim—sigh a lot, bang things on occasion, and act in a manner that says "Can't you see how unhappy I am?" Phil manipulates her by being passive-aggressive. He "gets around" to doing things she asks but in his time, not when it's most convenient for her. He tries to make her feel guilty for all the work he does around the house when she thinks it's his responsibility to bear half the load anyway. Finally Toni decides to talk.

TONI: You didn't kiss me goodbye this morning.

PHIL: I forgot.

TONI: You forget a lot of things. Remember I asked you to repair the light switch in the hallway? It's been weeks.

PHIL: It's not like I've been watching TV all this time.

TONI: It's just that I feel you do what you want and don't really pay attention to me.

(This is getting off to a rough start. If she tries to pick apart everything that bothers her, Phil will feel attacked. Better to open with something less accusatory and get to the heart of the matter quickly.)

TONI: Let me start over. I don't want to sound so critical. I've noticed that when I think you're being uncooperative, I try to get even in small ways. Maybe you've seen me moping around and acting unhappy.

PHIL: Yes.

TONI: I'm hoping you can admit that you do similar things to me.

PHIL: I stay out of your way. That's what I do.

TONI: Like when you didn't kiss me goodbye this morning.

PHIL: I guess I do it to annoy you and avoid an argument.

TONI: Thank you for admitting that. Another thing I've noticed is that when I have to ask you repeatedly to do something for me, you try to make me feel guilty when you're the one who's made promises he didn't keep.

PHIL: Not always.

TONI: True. But I'd really appreciate it if you would go with the spirit of this conversation. I'm saying we each do things to displease the other when we're angry and not able to talk about what's bothering us.

(This is a good example of trying to stay on track. The point is not to debate facts about certain events but to recognize that they each can be manipulative.)

PHIL: When I complain to you, I think you get defensive, like I'm not supposed to feel the way I do. That's why I'd rather not talk.

TONI: Like when you're annoyed that I don't feel like having sex?

PHIL: Right. Good example. You make me feel I'm wrong to want it.

(This is a good place for Toni to say to herself, "I accept my spouse is blaming me right now and not looking at his contribution to the problem." Acceptance will tone down her annoyance.)

TONI: You're right. I have done that and I shouldn't. But I do it because it's connected to how I think you treat me overall. You make me feel I'm wrong to want you to fix a light switch. I try to be patient, give you all the time you want. Then you don't follow up and I'm the bad guy for complaining. I think we each make each other feel guilty.

PHIL: I see that.

TONI: Aren't you tired of being aggravated with me so much?

PHIL: Yeah. What can we do to fix it?

(Good. The conversation is getting to the "what to do" part. That happens more quickly and effortlessly when there are no stubborn debates and each side is willing to admit mistakes.)

TONI: Somehow we have to be willing to speak up more rather than communicate indirectly.

PHIL: But what if I speak up and still don't get what I want?

TONI: But what if you do? And what if I don't get what I want? We have to be willing to stop looking at a conversation as having a winner and a loser. Sometimes we get our way, sometimes we don't, and sometimes we compromise.

PHIL: Let's give it a try and see what happens.

As you can see, when each partner can admit wrongdoing rather than blaming the other, the chances of having a successful conversation improve dramatically.

"We need
to talk"

Chapter Four

Friends and Family

IMAGINE THAT SOME members of your spouse's family aren't
people you would ordinarily want to accompany you on a vacation. Do you roll your eyes when you think about your spouse's
friends? What if there has been some bad blood between you and
an in-law and your spouse wants you to cast aside your resentments
for the sake of family unity? Even if no ill-will exists, relating to
a spouse's family or friends often involves making sacrifices and
putting up with people and situations that can be stressful and, at
times, aggravating.

Why Can't We All Just Get Along?

People usually feel at ease when their thoughts, feelings, and actions
are all aligned and consistent with one another. For example, a
spouse who thinks "It's important to be on good terms with my in-
laws" and has the corresponding feeling "I really enjoy my in-laws,"
and then acts on those thoughts and feelings by spending pleasant time with them, will feel content. On the other hand, imagine
a woman who understands that getting along with her in-laws is
important but who finds them objectionable (her thoughts and
emotions are misaligned). Or think of her husband whose thoughts

dictate he should stand by his wife *and* be loyal to his family but who cannot act both ways consistently because loyalty to one party is viewed as disloyalty by the other party (his thoughts are not able to align with his actions).

Imagine a vertical line running down the midline of your body. That represents an alignment between your head (thoughts), heart (feelings), and legs (actions). If the line isn't straight, you'll be twisted like a pretzel and not very happy. Most thorny relationship problems remain thorny because people cannot cope well when their thoughts, feelings, and behaviors are at odds ("I should do this, but I don't want to . . .").

Relationship Strain—The Different Players

Relationship strain with in-laws is common. Sometimes a spouse doesn't dislike the in-laws but believes his or her partner is too involved with them (and therefore underinvolved at home). "You always jump when your Dad asks for some help around the house but you never get around to fixing the things I've asked for," and so on. There is no hard-and-fast rule about what constitutes a too-close relationship with one's parents, friends, or siblings. You are probably overinvolved with your parents (or others) if:

- You cannot say no to them, or saying no makes you feel extremely guilty.
- Your parents have too much say over where you reside or how you and your spouse raise your children.
- You speak more often to your parents (or siblings or friends) about your marital issues than you do to your spouse.
- They are allowed to drop by unannounced at any time for any reason, instead of calling ahead at least once in a while.

- You spend more quality time with them than you do with your spouse.

Even if you get along famously with your in-laws or spouse's friends, there will be times when you will object, perhaps strenuously, to your partner spending time with them. Since this issue will likely never go away completely, you must be prepared to have repeated conversations about it—not to fix the problem once and for all but to manage it more effectively. When you manage a problem, you expect it to recur—much like having to change your work schedule to accommodate a sick child or sending your car to the shop periodically for needed repairs. Thus, the conversation is not littered with exclamations as to why this is happening (since it is expected to happen), but instead focuses on how to best deal with it this time around.

Good Openings

The right words don't have to be precise in order to be helpful. Your goal isn't to memorize a list of effective phrases but to get a feel for what effective phrases sound like when you have to inevitably think on your feet.

The best opening phrases start up gently—not harshly—and introduce the topic in a way that leads to teamwork and problem-solving, not defensiveness and debate. Your overall goal in the discussion is not to win and get your way but to at least understand one another with acceptance and perhaps to come up with ideas to address the problem to mutual satisfaction.

- "I know it's a sensitive subject but I'd really like us to find a way to deal with the issues I have with your family."

- "The holidays will be here soon and I'd like to figure out what our plans will be for family get-togethers. I want to be fair but I do have some concerns."
- "I'd like to talk about your family and what we can do to deal with the fact that I feel a lot of tension when I'm with them. Please bear with me."
- "This is hard to discuss but it would mean a lot to me if we can try to better understand each other's feelings about the ongoing problems I'm having with your family."
- "I know your friends are important to you and I'm not asking you to give them up, but I'd like us to figure out a way we can argue less often about the time you spend with them."
- "Your parents will be here this weekend. I want the weekend to go as well as it can but I need to discuss how to handle things when the usual difficulties arise."

As you can see, each opening remark started gently and then quickly got to the point about what the speaker hopes to accomplish during the conversation. If opening comments are vague or don't get to the bottom line quickly, the listener will get defensive or nervous about what's coming next. Also, comments such as "bear with me" and "I know your friends are important to you" demonstrate that the speaker has some sensitivity to the potential impact the conversation might have on the listener. That makes it easier (but there is no guarantee) for the listener to want to respond back with equal sensitivity.

Not-So-Good Openings
- "If your mother makes any more nasty comments about our home when she visits this weekend, I'm warning you I will give

it right back to her." (This invites debate, like a swordsman yelling *en guard*.)

- "I'm sick of you always defending your family and making me the bad guy."
- "I'm not going to the party if your parents (friends) will be there." (Opening remarks should invite a dialogue that clarifies each other's point of view instead of throwing down the gauntlet.)
- "Do whatever you want. What do I care?" (This isn't a discussion but a "why bother" comment where resentment will surface later.)

Good Follow-Throughs

Once the opening words are successfully spoken, a slightly tougher job is ahead. No matter how well you say your opening comments, your spouse may wish to have none of it. Then it is essential that you not escalate the debate but instead maintain a dogged determination to hear your spouse out and convey the strong desire to be teammates on this issue, not adversaries.

Thus, the goal during the middle phase of touchy conversations is to keep emotions manageable and to aim for mutual understanding. Most problems occur at this phase, when the goal of being understood far outweighs the goal of trying to understand. If you can't convey to your spouse that you understand his or her concerns (or that you really *want* to understand), your spouse will either become more adamant and inflexible, or will withdraw with a "forget about it" attitude.

These comments show that you appreciate or are sensitive to your spouse's position once the conversation is underway:

- "I can see that it's really important to you that family members try to get along. *And* at the same time I have a hard time with certain members of your family." (Use the word *and* rather than *but*.)
- "I don't blame you for being upset that I don't really care for your family (friends) that much. *And* at the same time I'm not sure what to do differently that feels fair to me."
- "I'm sure it's no fun for you when we all get together and you can tell I'm not happy with your family."
- "We just see things differently and that makes it hard on both of us."
- "I know I cannot convince you that you're wrong and I'm just as certain you can't convince me that I'm wrong. *And* we still have to come up with a plan of action."

The next comments can help you to de-escalate an intensifying argument. Acknowledging the part of your spouse's viewpoint that makes sense to you or admitting it when you spoke out of line can help immediately ease the tension.

- "I shouldn't have said that. Let me try it again."
- "It would help me stay focused if we could lower the volume."
- "You're right when you say that holidays are an important time for families. . . . You're right when you say that sometimes we have to accept people's ways in order to just get along."

The ultimate purpose of the follow-through phase of conversation is to help you arrive at a place of mutual understanding and, if possible, to come up with a plan of action acceptable to each of you.

Not-So-Good Follow-Throughs

The key obstacles discussed in Chapter 1 that are most likely to rear their ugly heads here are the "should" mentality (for example, "You should find a way to get along better with my family" or "You should tell your mother off when she insults me like that") and the "but I'm right!" stance. Steer clear of them during this touchy conversation.

- "A husband should stand by his wife in those situations." (Better: "I feel alone when you don't defend me.")
- "I will never feel warm toward your family." "I'll never like your friends." (Better: "I wouldn't choose them as my family/closest friends but I think we can figure out a way to help the situation be less tense for both of us.")
- "That's right, put everyone else first and me last." (Better: "I want to feel that I'm important to you and that my concerns about this matter to you. Can we figure out a way for each of us to feel a little better about this situation?")

Check Your SAIL

When touchy conversations go off-track, usually one or both spouses feel hurt, misunderstood, or disrespected. Learning to speak more gently and trying to seek common ground may be all that is needed to get back on-track. That is the "S" in SAIL. Once a conversation starts to implode, immediately change your tone to a normal speaking level and find something positive to say about your spouse's viewpoints.

Accept Versus Judge

Now it is time to examine your willingness to "accept" your spouse's thoughts and feelings without harsh judgment. Imagine having the conversation about your dislike for your spouse's family and imagine that your spouse defends his or her family. Will you fight that or accept it? To accept it does not mean you won't try to better explain your point of view. It simply means that you will not emotionally oppose your spouse's viewpoint for two reasons. First, you are unlikely to talk him or her out of it by intense verbal persuasion. Second, trying to do so will probably add to the polarization of your opinions and make it harder to feel like a team. Lack of acceptance places you squarely in the quicksand that "should" thinking almost always brings about. You are essentially reacting with this sentiment: "I cannot accept what you think or feel about this issue because you shouldn't be thinking or feeling that way anyway." You have therefore closed off your listening and your spouse will regard you as inflexible or controlling and he or she will try to make *that* the issue. It is better to tell yourself, "I wish my spouse felt the way I do about this matter, but I accept that is not the case."

Inquire Further

The "I" in SAIL asks you to inquire for the possible deeper issue underlying the surface issue. The fact that a deeper issue may exist does not diminish the importance of the surface issue. However, a conversation that excludes an examination of the deeper issue may be unsatisfying and ineffective. When the conversation is stuck, try saying "Maybe there is more to this issue than meets the eye. Would you mind if we take a few minutes to explore that?" If your

Conversation Peace

Turn unpleasant family get-togethers into something fun—and even romantic—for you and your mate. For example, you might decide that every time one of you has to put up with something objectionable at a family gathering, the two of you will kiss publicly. No one will know why the two of you seem to be kissing so much—it will be your secret—and you will get a real kick out of playing with their minds.

spouse doesn't wish to do any exploring, you can add "Well, I'd like to see if something else is bothering me besides the fact that I don't like your family. I'm going to take a break to do that."

Possible underlying issues when you dislike your spouse's friends or family:

- I'm not important to him; otherwise he'd do things my way.
- This relationship isn't fair. My spouse always gets her way.
- I'm always putting aside my needs for the sake of others. When will it be my turn?
- We never have enough time together for just ourselves, so I resent it when he spends time with his family or friends.
- My last partner took me for granted. I think my spouse is doing the same thing.

Once you identify a possible underlying issue or theme, it's a good idea to introduce that into your discussion.

- "I guess it bothers me that I have to put up with your family and friends because most of my life it seems I have to go along with meeting other people's needs while my needs get neglected."
- "My brothers always teased me when I was a kid and my parents laughed it off. I guess I want you to take me seriously when I tell you that your family sometimes treats me disrespectfully."
- "If we had more time for ourselves together I probably wouldn't object so much to the time you spend with your friends (family)."

Create a List of Possible Actions

The "L" in SAIL suggests you begin making a list of possible actions that can be taken to help alleviate your mutual concerns. When you dislike your spouse's friends or family, effective action plans include ways to meet both of your needs. What can happen so that you spend time with your in-laws and at the same time feel more supported or understood by your spouse? Try to find a plan acceptable to you both. If you come up with a plan and your spouse doesn't like it, avoid comments such as "You're too inflexible. . . . You're not cooperating. . . . It's always your way," and so forth. Better to say, "Let's come up with a plan we are each willing to accomplish, even if we don't agree with it wholeheartedly."

| Sample Script | "We need to talk" |

Kate can't get along with her husband Jim's family, especially his sister, and was adamant about not attending yet another family birthday party—the third get-together in a month. Jim was just as adamant that Kate needed to make the best of the situation. Here is a piece of their original unsuccessful conversation:

JIM: Everyone in my family thinks you hate them. No wonder they act tense around you.

KATE: Why can't you back me up once in a while? Why must I make all the concessions while your family gets to insult me or ignore me whenever they feel like it?

JIM: You're overreacting. And what am I supposed to do, divorce my family?

On the surface, this has all the makings of a potential disaster. Jim thinks Kate is oversensitive and uncooperative. Kate feels that Jim is disloyal by siding against her. It is a good example of one of the perpetual, there-is-no-perfect-solution types of problem discussed in Chapter 1. Eventually, Jim and Kate settled this area of conflict. Here is how their successful conversation looked:

JIM: I hate to be the bearer of bad news but we're invited to my nephew's thirteenth birthday party. Everyone will be there.

KATE: Another birthday party? That's the third get-together this month. I'm sorry Jim but I'm going to take a pass. You know I don't feel comfortable with your family, especially your sister Carol.

(He began the conversation gently which was good. Kate responded by apologizing that she didn't want to go. At this point they are disagreeing without being disagreeable.)

JIM: But this birthday is for Carol's son. She will take it personally if you don't show up.

KATE: I'm not going.

(They are each starting to draw lines in the sand. Unless they correct it, the conversation will turn into a debate and then an argument.)

JIM: My family already thinks you hate them.

KATE: What's more important? What your family thinks or what I think? Wait, I'm sorry. I know it's no fun for you that I don't really get along with your side of the family.

(Kate successfully de-escalated the discussion by admitting it wasn't helpful to paint Jim into a corner.)

JIM: No it isn't fun for me. But I know my family takes no prisoners and they can be pretty rude.

(Jim responds to Kate's de-escalation by validating her feelings—a common response to an apology. Now they each are starting to feel understood.)

JIM: But I still want you to go. My family won't understand it if you don't. They'll see right through any excuse we make.

KATE: I get that. But if I go this time—for your sake—what about the next time and the time after that? Will there ever be a time you'd be okay with me staying home?

(Kate "accepted" Jim's wish that she attend anyway. Kate didn't object since she realized that Jim was simply expressing his wishes. If she'd pounced on his words and told him he was wrong to feel that way, he'd have become frustrated.)

JIM: This problem will never go away completely.

KATE: I agree. And I don't want to fight about it every time it comes up.

JIM: So what do we do?

KATE: Is there something else that's bothering you about this situation?

(Kate is inquiring about what is really important.)

JIM: I feel that you should overlook my family's ways—all the rest of us do—and not take things so personally.

KATE: That's your idea of a solution. What I want to know is what bothers you.

(Kate did not get sidetracked. She knew that no solution would work unless each of them was able to really clarify what the issue is that's bothering them the most.)

JIM: Well, I guess I don't want to be the cause of any family tension. I hate confrontations. Life is too short. My mother won't live forever. My sister isn't a happy person. I don't want us to get added to her list of problems.

KATE: I understand that. But this is what bothers me: When you ask me to overlook your family's difficult ways, I feel like my feelings don't count to you.

JIM: I know. But if the only way I can prove to you that you matter to me and that your feelings count is to go along with something that will make me miserable, I don't think we win in the long run.

KATE: Right. So the question is, how can I start to believe that my feelings matter to you without you having to feel like you're creating more tension with your family?

(They have successfully shifted from a competition where for one to win the other must lose, and are now seeking common ground.)

KATE: I need a plan that allows me some freedom to not attend certain family functions.

JIM: And I need you to try to overlook some things my family does that will probably never change.

KATE: Like how they tease a person mercilessly when there is a small mishap?

JIM: Right.

KATE: Will you defend me in their presence if they do something really mean?

JIM: Well, I don't think they've ever been really mean but yes, I'll do that.

KATE: What will you say?

JIM: I guess I'll tell them that I love you and it bothers me when they say those things.

KATE: I would love that.

JIM: But I won't get in their face about it. No big confrontations.

KATE: That's fine. It would also be great if you said nice things about me in their presence. Just sprinkle that in your conversations.

JIM: Okay. That's easy.

This issue may not be solved once and for all, but they are now able to handle the conversation better the next time the issue will inevitably arise.

Chapter Five

Adversity

IF YOU LOVE hard enough or live long enough you will eventually endure some type of misfortune or loss. A couple's world can get turned upside down in an instant when they hear bad news. The most common hardships include health problems, financial setbacks, or the death of a loved one. During hard or scary times couples will either grow more connected or less connected. Rarely does their level of connectedness remain the same as it was before the hardship.

If there is ever a time when the phrase "we need to talk" applies, it is when the couple is coping with adversity. Ironically, that is the time when conversations can be clumsy and quarrelsome—or avoided altogether.

The Marriage Immune System

When your physical immune system is strong and balanced, you are more able to fight off illness and recover faster from injuries. An unbalanced immune system can both overfunction (as it does in the case of allergies) or underfunction (as it does when an infection persists). The degree of your marital satisfaction affects your "emotional" immune system. People with overreactive emotional immune systems are too sensitive and can become anxious or depressed more quickly, or take things too personally and become argumentative. Those with an underreactive emotional immune system are too insensitive and may be in denial about the seriousness of an issue or are slow to respond when action is called for.

It is typically the case that married partners are not identical when it comes to their coping styles. Depending upon the issue, one partner is likely to be more talkative, more anxious, or more withdrawn than the other. In other words, during adversity one partner may wish to connect while the other may wish to have space. The couple then gets into a slight tug-of-war, each one trying to prod the other into behaving a certain way. If the difference between the spouses is great, each one feels more lonely and misunderstood in the process.

Coping with the Situation Versus Coping with Your Feelings about the Situation

During a family crisis, or any kind of adversity, a person must contend with two factors: practical steps to deal with the problem at hand (the "fix it" focus) and steps to bring about emotional balance (the "how do I feel about what's happening?" focus). Once two people are involved, they sometimes trade off who will focus on what aspect of the problem. As a result, one spouse may be very problem-focused (making sure things get done and the problem is being tackled—usually the husband) while the other spouse (usually the wife) is more emotion-focused (trying to make sure that feelings are not ignored). So for example, if money is very tight and one spouse takes on two jobs to make ends meet, the other may then complain that quality family time is lacking. While such an arrangement makes it look like all bases are now covered, this will become a divisive issue if the hard times linger (such as an inability to find a job after six months of searching) or if the problem is chronic (such as a permanent or long-standing health issue). For a short-term crisis, it's fine if one spouse is the emotionally aloof (less empathic) problem solver and the other is the emotional soother, but those roles will not stand up over time. To function well over the long haul, each spouse must possess both styles.

A Man's Default Drive

Under stress, men (or whoever is more "bottom line"-oriented in the relationship) tend to shift into "do" mode. They want to look for answers to fix the problem. If the problem is not fixable right away, men look for ways to stay busy or preoccupied. They usually downplay their softer side. Their instinct is to protect and provide, not hold their partner close and converse. Talking about how they feel is harder for many men during periods of crisis. They also feel uneasy listening to their wives talk about their feelings. To a man, feelings are problems to be solved. He prefers to think and mull things over rather than talk things out, and therefore can come across as distant or uncaring. If he can't do anything about a certain problem (say, a loved one is in the hospital having a serious operation) he might prefer to go to work and stay busy rather than sit in a waiting room with nothing to do. Or if his wife is very scared or preoccupied about some serious issue, her husband might clean out her car or repaint a room or get busy with some chore—all done as his way to show her he cares. To her, it may seem like he is putting less important things ahead of her.

In fact, when men act that way they are emotionally flooded. They cope with those emotions by distracting themselves and pushing their feelings aside. Allowing themselves to feel and express emotions such as fear makes them feel out of control. During stressful times, a man may try to connect with his wife more through touch than talk. Sex becomes his main avenue for feeling close to his wife.

A Woman's Default Drive

Women (or whoever is more emotionally open) tend to be more feeling-focused and relationship-focused during stressful times. Her instinct is to strive for togetherness. She makes sure that not only is the problem at hand being addressed, but the emotional consequences of that problem are not overlooked. If a problem cannot be solved by conversation, men tend to be less interested in talking while women see the value of talking as an end in itself. Whereas many men need to mull things over by themselves to determine how they feel and what they want to do, a woman often prefers to talk things out in order to clarify how she feels. This can result in a pattern of relating where one spouse pursues the other for greater intimacy and closeness and the other tries to carve out space and distance. The man (or whoever is the more emotionally distant partner) may eventually view his wife as too emotional and needy. She will regard him as too cold. Neither claim is wholly accurate. Under stress, couples tend to become more polarized as each spouse resorts to a more extreme version of their natural style of coping.

The push and pull that couples experience when they try to force a way of coping on the other will only add to the stress they are under and result in disenchantment. Communicating during difficult times is not about getting one's way. It's not about insisting that the quiet spouse talk more or insisting that the talkative spouse remain quiet. It's about how to manage those differences in coping—not eliminate them—so that you feel more connected as a couple.

Halting the Battle of Wills

To briefly summarize, as a couple going through some sort of hard time, it's important to have emotional access to each other—closeness improves the overall emotional immune system. Often, differences in coping styles become exaggerated during a time of crisis or emotional upheaval. As a result, it's harder to feel connected since one partner may require more emotional space than the other. This can lead to a battle of wills, which only makes matters worse. Ultimately, each spouse must find a way to yield to the other's wishes to some degree—and to do so willingly, not under duress. That means the battle of wills must cease and the couple must be able to meet each other halfway. That requires an ability to talk about what needs to happen.

Many well-intended spouses are reluctant to say what's on their mind during a stressful period due to numerous fears or concerns. The top fears are:

1. **Fear of making the spouse more upset.** When anxiety is high it is more likely that a spouse's emotion-laden comments will trigger defensiveness, disagreement, or simply discomfort. Usually the culprit is a difficulty accepting a spouse's emotional reactions. If the goal becomes trying to *understand* instead of trying to *fix*, it's easier to tolerate it when a spouse's emotions are running high during a stressful period.

2. **Fear of saying the wrong thing.** Sometimes, all you want to do is help a spouse feel better, but many well-intended conversations end up with one spouse saying,

    "I can't believe you just said that!" and the other defensively responding "But I'm only trying to help!" The culprit here is once again an inability to accept a spouse's comments (the "A" in SAIL) and a failure to give the benefit of the doubt or cut the partner some slack.

3. **Fear of losing emotional control.** Often, it's a fear of one's own emotional reaction that is problematic. Men especially (or anyone who has a strong need to feel in control of his or her emotions) are prone to avoiding emotional discussions for fear of becoming emotional themselves. The culprit here is—you guessed it—lack of acceptance. When spouses can accept the fact that they may react with emotion and not feel a pressure to suppress it (assuming the reaction is nonviolent), conversations are less likely to be avoided.

Once you understand the reasons why you think and feel the way you do during stressful times, the next step is to climb over those hurdles and talk in a manner that will be helpful to you and your spouse.

Dialogue Dos

All of the rules and tips mentioned so far in this book certainly should be kept in mind when talking to your spouse during periods of crisis or adversity. However, some additional key points need to be mentioned—especially during an unexpected crisis—because it is during such times that people can fly off the handle or crawl into a corner and shut down. Even couples with a strong relationship can make harsh criticisms in the heat of the moment during a crisis.

For example, Larry was waiting in the veterinarian's office when his wife called him on his cell phone. Janet was frantic. A wintry mix of ice and rain had made roads slippery and their daughter Jamie was involved in a car accident. She was injured, though it wasn't life-threatening. An ambulance was on its way. Larry raced from the vet's office to go to the scene of the accident, which was only ten minutes away. However, the road conditions were bad and other accidents had forced detours. A half hour had passed and he still hadn't arrived. Janet called him.

"Why aren't you there yet?" she demanded.

"I'm doing the best I can," he shouted back. "Traffic is all jammed up."

"Didn't you think to take a detour?" Janet said. "Jamie needs one of us there. Don't you understand that?"

"I'm not stupid, of course I understand that!" Larry said.

Fear had taken over and their conversation, like Jamie's car, had skidded off course. Even later on, when Jamie was home safely, Larry and Janet's conversations were punctuated with hostility.

"I told you Jamie was too inexperienced to drive in bad weather," Larry said.

"How is she supposed to get experience?" Janet answered. "Besides, the storm was unexpected. It's not my fault it happened while Jamie was out driving."

Larry and Janet's anxiety over the events of the day caused some old divisive issues to surface. It's a common theme during adversity: If something goes wrong, someone is to blame. However, during highly stressful times, couples should do their best to accomplish the following:

Turn toward one another, not against or away.

Fundamentally, couples relate to each other in three ways: they turn toward one another (connect); they turn against one another (clash); or turn away from each other (disconnect). In periods of crisis, clashing or disconnecting happens more than it should. When you have a moment to reflect, ask yourself if you have moved toward your partner enough during the stressful moments. If you haven't, make efforts now to repair that and try to be more aware the next time emotions get heated.

Say such things as: "How are you managing? Anything you need right now? We'll get through this. These things aren't easy."

Don't say: "Can't you see I need time for myself right now? This is your fault. Stay out of my way and let me handle this."

Don't take it personally.

Be tolerant of the fact that your spouse (and you) might be overemotional or perhaps argumentative during a frightening event. Try not to hold it against your spouse if his or her reaction upsets you. Also, be tolerant of the fact that your spouse might appear to be underemotional, as well. What comes across as coldness or indifference may be that person's way of keeping their emotions in check and not losing emotional control.

Say such things as: "I don't blame you for feeling upset. . . . I know you're angry but we're on the same team. . . . Bear with me, I'm not thinking clearly right now. . . . I didn't mean to sound harsh. . . . I appreciate your calmness."

Don't say: "How dare you raise your voice at me. . . . I can't believe you're speaking to me this way. You must not care, otherwise you'd. . . ."

Look for the fear that's behind negative emotional expression.
During a crisis, any angry outburst is fueled by fear, and people say and do things they'd never think of doing otherwise. Even the "calm and collected" spouse is probably worried. It's easier to tolerate a spouse's emotional reaction in a crisis when you understand that he or she is simply afraid and trying hard to cope. During adversity, the angry person is actually scared underneath. The guilt-ridden person is scared. The worried person is scared. The depressed person feels both scared and helpless.

Say such things as: "I hear that you're angry but I know you're also scared. . . . We're both feeling many emotions right now, and the main one is we're afraid. . . . What scares you the most right now? . . . What would help to make you feel less afraid?"

Don't say: "You have no right to be angry with me. . . . You're so quiet, don't you have any feelings at all? . . . There's nothing to be afraid of. . . . You always think the worst."

Good Openings
It doesn't matter if you're reading this chapter hoping to find a way to talk about a specific kind of hardship or adversity such as cancer, the death of a loved one, a serious injury, a major financial setback,

and so forth. This chapter can help you in all cases. While the specific words of a conversation will vary depending upon the situation, it is the emotional content that is key. Couples who carry on helpful conversations during a time of crisis use words that manage their emotions. When it comes to finding the right words, the topic at hand is less important than the way that topic is discussed.

In a sudden crisis, focus more on what happened and what needs to happen next. Don't focus much on how or why it happened if you need to be taking action. You can deal with that later.

- "I received some news today about _____. I'm scared and I want us to figure out what we can do." (This is helpful because it frames the discussion narrowly—trying to figure out what needs to happen.)
- "I got a call that your dad had a heart attack and is in the hospital. I don't know any more details. I'll be by to pick you up. Will you be okay until then?" (This is to the point, presents a plan of action, and shows sensitivity to the other person.)
- "I was laid off from work today. I'm worried we won't pay our bills. I need us to figure things out." (The most productive discussions balance out the need for a practical plan of action with the need to express feelings and be understood.)

If the hardship is chronic but the immediate crisis has passed, couples still have to contend with the long-term consequences of what happened. Emotions may be more subdued than when the problem first occurred, but they are still a factor and must not be overlooked simply because time has passed and some degree of adjustment has happened.

Conversation Peace

If tensions are escalating during a serious crisis despite efforts to get your spouse to calm down, stop debating and give your spouse permission to be emotional. Say things like, "It's all-right if you get upset now. It's okay to yell, I can't blame you for being worried. You have a right to be scared." Most people who are getting out of control calm down when they feel understood and accepted.

- "I notice you seem quieter as we get closer to the anniversary of your mom's passing. Anything I can do?" (This is helpful because the spouse didn't wait for an invitation to bring up the topic.)
- "I can't go with you today. My back pain is too severe. I'm sorry. We can make plans for some other time or you can go ahead and I'll be fine here." (When someone has chronic and disabling pain, plans often have to be cancelled at the last minute, which can be frustrating for the healthier spouse. Showing understanding for the sacrifices that spouse must make is always a good idea.)
- "It must be frustrating that you can't get in or out of bed without help." (When someone "adjusts" to their disability, they still can feel bothered or upset from time to time. Often, other family members forget that, and assume that if the person isn't speaking up and complaining they must be okay. Often they are simply keeping feelings to themselves.)

Good Follow-Throughs

The follow-through is where things get most complicated. It's easy for emotions to escalate quickly under stress and create even more strain for the couple. Follow-through words should first and foremost help manage emotions. Trying to figure out how to handle the crisis gets too cumbersome if emotions are out of control.

- "I know you are upset, but I need you to lower your voice and speak more slowly so I can listen better." (Listening and understanding is more important than coming up with an action plan. Without an adequate understanding, any plan may be ineffective.)
- "I know you're trying to help but I just want you to understand my feelings, not provide answers." (It's essential that you inform your partner what you need from the conversation.)
- "I know you're worried that things could get much worse, and I'm trying to remain optimistic. Can we just accept that neither of us knows for sure what will happen and that we'll have to deal with it when it comes?" (It's smart to avoid a no-win debate.)
- "We're both upset and wanting to find someone to blame. Can we talk about that later? Right now I just need to deal with what's happening." (In a scary crisis such as a medical emergency when a child is seriously injured or there was a car accident, one person may try to blame the other for carelessness. That will only invite debate and stir hard feelings. Fault-finding is common but it is fueled by fear—not necessarily truth and objectivity.)
- "I appreciate it that we can talk calmly." (Saying "thank you" is always a good idea.)

Sample Script

"We need to talk"

Erin was three months pregnant when she suffered a miscarriage. It was her second miscarriage in as many pregnancies. She and Chris were heartbroken and scared that they may never have a child. A few days had passed. Chris returned to work while Erin stayed home for an extra week. Their emotions were raw. In the hours immediately following the loss, Chris tried to be optimistic. That only made Erin mad.

"You make it sound so easy, that we can get pregnant again and have our baby. But that doesn't happen to us. Haven't you figured that out?" Erin said.

Chris suggested that Erin call her mom for extra support. Erin interpreted that as Chris's way of becoming unavailable. "No," Chris countered. "I just want you to feel better."

"Well I don't see *you* calling anybody for support," Erin said. "Doesn't it bother you what happened?"

Chris was flabbergasted that Erin would say such a thing. A few days later they were able to have the conversation they should have had from the beginning. It still had its awkward moments—but they corrected those errors as quickly as possible.

ERIN: I feel like we may never have children.

CHRIS: We don't know that for sure.

ERIN: (A bit sarcastically) Well, I wish I had your optimism.

CHRIS: Neither of us expected a miscarriage after three months.

(Chris didn't take it personally when Erin was sarcastic. Instead his comments told her that her feelings made sense.)

ERIN: What makes you seem so hopeful?

CHRIS: The doctors are telling us to keep trying. They haven't given up so we shouldn't either.

ERIN: I don't know.

CHRIS: I don't know either. (He puts his arm around her.)

ERIN: I feel so helpless. And I keep thinking I must have done something wrong; that I didn't take care of myself well enough.

CHRIS: I don't believe that. These things happen.

ERIN: Please don't talk to me like I'm twelve. I know these things happen. I just don't know why they keep happening to *us.*

CHRIS: What do you want me to say? I don't want you to be so down on yourself but if I try to make you feel better you get upset with me. I'm unhappy, too, you know.

ERIN: You don't show it.

(If they are listening to each other closely, they have redefined the problem. Chris is frustrated he can't "fix" Erin. She's frustrated that his emotions are held in check.)

CHRIS: Maybe that's how I deal with the things I can't change. I just try to focus on the future.

ERIN: That's not how I deal with things. Maybe we're not compatible.

CHRIS: I can't believe you're talking like that.

(Up until now Chris has been trying to stay focused. Now he's getting annoyed. They run the risk of having an escalating argument. Erin senses this and now she is the one who de-escalates the conversation.)

ERIN: I'm sorry. I didn't mean that. I'm just so . . . upset.

CHRIS: Me too.

ERIN: What happened to your optimism?

CHRIS: It comes and goes. I'm optimistic we'll get through this but I don't know what exactly will happen and when. I'm still willing to paint the baby's bedroom.

ERIN: Maybe in a few weeks. Not right away.

CHRIS: Okay.

ERIN: Going back to work will be so hard . . . facing everybody . . . everyone being so sympathetic and asking how I'm doing.

CHRIS: Yeah.

(Chris stops himself from trying to tell her how to be less troubled by her return to work. Instead he just acknowledges her feelings. That's helpful.)

CHRIS: I'm not looking forward to all my coworkers asking me questions, either. I guess they'll stop asking soon enough.

ERIN: I want to try again and yet I don't. I'm afraid of it happening all over.

CHRIS: I know what you mean. And at the same time I want us to try. Someday in the future we won't be so focused on what happened this week.

ERIN: Someday.

Erin and Chris haven't solved their problems but have successfully found a way to manage their emotions while talking about a painful loss. As their conversation gets calmer and more supportive, they feel closer and more connected, despite their loss.

"We need to talk"

Chapter Six

Sex

IMAGINE SAYING THIS to your spouse: "I have some issues about our sexual relationship and I'd like us to figure out what we can do about that. Okay?"

Most people can't speak that way without their anxiety shooting up. Most likely they are afraid of hurting feelings or starting an argument, or afraid their spouse won't take them seriously. Maybe they feel embarrassed talking about sex, or they're afraid that the discussion will result in them feeling blamed or sexually inadequate.

Talking about Sex

This may surprise you but you may not have to talk about sex with your partner if it really scares you to do so. Instead, each of you can agree to read this chapter—maybe even point to those sections that are most important to you—and then see how much or how little you want to discuss matters. This chapter might do most of the talking for you.

Among the more common sexual issues:

- Reduced desire
- Disagreement on how often to make love—and when

- Too much or too little foreplay
- Sex has become routine and a tad boring
- Arousal difficulties
- Lack of cuddling or connection before or afterward
- Body image problems
- A wide variety of sexual disorders

And let's not forget personality factors. Many people pull away sexually from their spouse when they're angry, while others seek out their partner sexually (as a way to bring about closeness). Personal history can also play a role. People who felt unloved or rejected as a child may seek out a partner sexually in order to feel accepted, or they might withdraw—afraid to get too close in case they get hurt later on. Then there are those couples who sleep in separate

Conversation Peace

What's normal when it comes to sex within a marriage? According to a classic study in *The New England Journal of Medicine*, for couples in their thirties, about 25 to 30 percent will report occasional sexual dissatisfaction and half will report occasional disinterest in sex. About half of your love-making encounters will be very satisfying and half will be less so—at least for one of you—though not necessarily unsatisfying. By the time a man turns fifty he will report occasional arousal difficulties (which require additional stimulation or novelty to reduce the rate of sluggishness). The average couple (across all ages) has sex a little more than once a week. About 10 percent have sex once a month or less.

beds because they work different shifts, have medical limitations, or contend with annoyances such as excessive snoring. There are also fears of pregnancy, alcohol-related sexual performance issues, sexual secrets (a hidden affair, embarrassing sexual desires), age-related sexual changes, and medication side-effects. The different possible scenarios are endless.

You're Not Alone

Just about every couple will—sooner or later—mumble to themselves that things aren't as hot in the sex department as they once were. For some, it's manageable. For others, it can be a troublesome disappointment. Sexual problems don't have to be cause for concern. The way that a couple deals with their sexual differences has more impact on the marriage than whatever the sexual difficulties are.

Talking Dirty—Or No Talking at All

The number-one way people assent to having sex is nonverbally. A little kissing, a little groping, maybe some slight wishy-washy resistance by one partner coupled with some probing perseverance by the other, and then it happens. And during sex, most if not all communication is also nonverbal. Lovers give signals that they want more of this or less of that and at any point in time one person might take the lead, as in a dance. All that nonverbal communication makes people feel self-conscious when a real conversation needs to happen.

Another key reason that talking about sex can increase tension is when the conversation isn't really about sex—it just seems that way. People take sexual problems personally and sexual problems quickly can mushroom into ego problems. So the sex talk is sometimes really about how to feel competent, attractive, desirable, lovable, or powerful. That's what often underlies a touchy conversation about sex and that's what often *isn't* adequately discussed.

The bulk of sexual concerns couples experience can be narrowed into two areas: low or mismatched desire; and performance problems. Take this quiz:

"We need

Answer True or False.

1. *I wish there'd be more caressing and tenderness during sex.*
2. *I'd rather not discuss sexual concerns.*
3. *I wish we had more "quickies."*
4. *If I was troubled by sexual performance I'd avoid or limit sex.*
5. *Sex for us is too often about "getting off" and very genitally focused.*
6. *Arousal difficulties make me upset or very anxious.*
7. *I enjoy erotica as a way to lead into sex.*
8. *I can enjoy sex even if I'm not fully aroused or "into it."*
9. *If I had a choice between a sexual encounter or a romantic encounter, I'd choose a romantic one.*
10. *If I had some performance problems that continued, I'd be more than willing to speak to a physician.*
11. *I wish I could have sex three times a week or more.*
12. *I can emotionally accept that sexual performance might change depending upon health and age.*

to talk"

Scoring:

If you answered **TRUE** to numbers one, five, and nine, you desire more affection, warmth, and romance in your physical relationship than you're now getting.

If you answered **TRUE** to numbers three, seven, and eleven, you like sex to focus more on the physical aspects rather than the emotional.

If you answered **TRUE** to numbers two, four, and six, you will likely avoid dealing with sexual concerns.

If you answered **TRUE** to numbers eight, ten, and twelve, you will be less anxious about sexual concerns that arise and more able to deal with them straightforwardly.

Whatever the sexual concern, the more anxious a spouse is about it and the more reluctant to address the issues, the more the problem will persist and the more likely it is that the problem will lead to frustration and ill-will in the marriage.

Low or Mismatched Desire

Mismatched sexual desire is the number-one sexual complaint among couples and if you think about it, that makes sense. It hardly seems reasonable that spouses would want to have sex at the same frequency and be ready and willing at the precise time a partner is ready. Too many other factors interfere, the most common being fatigue (childcare, home responsibilities, job stress) and relationship strain.

It isn't necessarily true that if you have low desire something must be wrong. The sexual drive is a basic drive but so is eating. Ever not feel hungry even though you hadn't eaten in a while and aren't sick? Basic drives can fluctuate. If you are someone who enjoys having sex about once a month and your spouse has the same desire, you don't have a problem you need to fix. If you like sex once a week and your spouse likes it three times a week, you have a problem. But the problem isn't low desire or high desire, it's mismatched desire.

Of course, low desire can indicate a problem especially if it's not what you or your spouse want. The main reasons for low desire are:

- Biological—medication side effects, health problems, hormonal fluctuations, and alcohol abuse.
- Personal—stress, depression, emotional trauma, and fatigue.
- Relational—marital strain or unhappiness, lack of affection, frequent arguing, or emotional detachment.

*(Someone who has had very low or no sexual desire all their adult life should see a health care professional.)

When low desire worsens or remains stubbornly the same despite efforts to make improvements, the manner in which the couple has dealt with the issue is likely doing more harm than good. For example, the higher-sex-drive partner usually displays patience and tolerance for a while and then feels entitled to have sex. But the lower-sex-drive partner resists that sexual pressure and ill-will results. Or the low-sex-drive partner may flinch or be unresponsive to affection, fearing that a positive response will invite unwanted sex. The affectionate partner feels hurt and rejected. Finally, a low-sex-drive partner might relent to having sex but the whole thing feels insincere or forced and sex is further avoided. It isn't long before each partner blames the other for being selfish or inconsiderate.

Men with Low Desire

Men and women can have low desire for very similar reasons. However, a common reason a man loses sexual desire is due to performance anxiety. He probably had one or more experiences in bed where he was unable to get an erection easily or he lost his erection too soon (or he experienced either premature or delayed ejaculation). That made him anxious. Anxiety interferes with sexual arousal and can create a self-fulfilling prophecy where sluggish arousal creates anxiety, which creates more arousal problems, and so on. (Also, men who view a lot of pornography, are having affairs, are under constant stress, or who don't get enough regular sleep can lose sexual interest in their spouse.)

Reduced levels of testosterone can also reduce a man's sex drive. However, while testosterone injections may improve desire, they won't necessarily improve the quality of physical arousal.

A final reason for low arousal is chronic, suppressed anger at one's wife. Usually, the anger has to do with feeling overburdened, underappreciated, and overcriticized. This can make a man feel emasculated. No doubt many wives believe their criticisms are warranted. However, phrasing comments in a positive way can be helpful. For example, instead of saying "We never go out anywhere," a wife might say "I really enjoyed being with you when we went to the movies a few weeks ago." Instead of complaining "The hole in the wall still isn't fixed!" she might say "I don't often tell you how grateful I am for all the work you do around the house. I don't know what I'd do without you."

Men are more likely to avoid conflict (and suppress emotions) than women. Therefore it's important that women present themselves as someone safe to talk to. But when conflicts go unresolved many women fail to follow the "S" in the SAIL approach to communication and begin difficult conversations more harshly—thereby making the situation worse. It can be helpful for men with low sexual desire to separate affection from sex. That way, they won't be worried that if they show affection it will be misinterpreted as a prelude to sex. Improving nonsexual areas of intimacy (talking, doing things together) can also improve closeness and perhaps increase sexual desire over time.

Women with Low Desire

More women than men report low sexual desire. Part of the reason can be hormonal. But the typical culprit for a woman's low sexual desire, psychologically speaking, is the quality of the marital relationship. Women need to feel loved in order to want to make love with a spouse. If women are fatigued and don't think their spouse is as helpful as he could be with chores or childcare, sex drives will plummet. When making love is all about getting to the meat and potatoes with no appetizer, many women feel taken for granted.

I often tell a husband who wishes his wife had a stronger desire for sex two things. First, if you want sex on Friday night, foreplay starts on Wednesday—and it isn't sexual foreplay I'm talking about. Make your wife feel loved and appreciated by small gestures, compliments, cooperation, and so on. Be understanding when she's tired, help her with things she ordinarily does by herself without having to be asked. If you have kids, take the kids out for a night to give her a break; don't complain if she wants a night out with her friends. Second, men need to increase the amount of nonsexual affection. Sexual affection is fine but men often do too much of that. It makes her feel desired but not necessarily beloved. Besides, if frequency of sex is an issue for you two, your sexual affections will look a lot like a come-on and just make her feel pressured. As a ballpark figure (since we men like numbers and keeping score), try to show nonsexual affection four times or more a day.

Performance Problems

Performance changes are inevitable. Performance "problems" are not. Many men believe that unless they remain fully erect at all times during a lovemaking encounter, something is wrong with their equipment. However, if lovemaking goes on for a longer duration and the man is focused on sensual foreplay that is not always genitally focused, he may not stay hard. That doesn't mean a thing unless he tells himself it is a serious issue. Intimate moments that are tender and low-energy can result in normal fluctuations in arousal. The key word is *normal*. (Arousal fluctuations do not necessarily indicate the man is not attracted to his wife or is disinterested in her.)

Men who are not nervous or appalled by fluctuating erections during sex usually focus on sexual play that doesn't call attention to the state of their penis. They might, for example, perform oral sex on their wife. Usually, their lack of anxiety about their erection status enables them to regain their erection fairly quickly.

Women can have performance concerns, too. Painful intercourse or inadequate lubrication can make sex a chore. The key in overcoming performance issues is to face the issue squarely, not avoid it. Whenever we avoid facing any fear, the fear gains in strength and becomes harder to overcome. Why? Because the relief you feel when you successfully escape or avoid a fearful situation is highly rewarding. Your brain wants to protect you from physical and psychological threat. If you believe that losing an erection is highly threatening to you, your brain will tell you to "run" and chemicals will be activated that will shut down your sexual responsiveness. There are helpful behavioral methods to overcome sexual difficulties. They are beyond the scope of this book but they involve the willingness to face the situation and learn to manage your anxiety during sexual moments.

Rules for Sex Talk

Like any touchy conversation, your goal is to bring forth concerns and suggest ways to deal with them, all the while showing respect and consideration for your partner's feelings and worries. If at any time the conversation gets rocky or tense, your fallback position should be to listen without challenging. Your goal then is to understand; not to judge, blame, or complain. Other points to keep in mind during sex talk:

- Remember that your partner's ego may be strongly connected to sexual functioning.
- Speak about what you'd like to see happen rather than complaining about what you don't like. (For example, saying "I'd like us to find a way to make love more often" is more helpful than "You don't seem to care about having sex.")
- Never shame your spouse over any sexual issue. ("Sex is all you ever think about.")
- Don't embrace the first solution that seems sensible ("Let's have sex once a week no matter what!") but brainstorm many ideas. Often, more than one idea may have to be used to address the issue since sex is a complicated subject.
- The most opportune time to talk about sexual concerns is right after you experience them. Waiting for the "right" time can be a long wait.

Good Openings

Raising sexual concerns almost always promotes defensiveness. Even if you start the discussion in a loving way, expect the conversation to be touchy. Whether you are discussing arousal problems, differences in desire, or differences in what turns you on, the emotional tone you set is key.

- "I don't expect us to always want the same amount of lovemaking, but I'm hoping we can come up with a plan that makes both of us more satisfied and less frustrated."
- "Yes, I'd like to make love more often and I can tell you would, too. Let's figure out some steps to take. Maybe we need more romance or more opportunity. What are your thoughts?"
- "Somehow we end up making each other feel bad about this. I don't want that."
- "I'm willing to listen to everything you have to say about this. I'm interested in what you think the source of the problem is."
- "When sex is avoided for whatever reason, I end up feeling less connected to you. I'm sure I can connect to you in other ways, but our sexual relationship is very important to me. I'm open to any ideas you have."

Good Follow-Throughs

The goal here is to manage your emotions during the dialogue so that the conversation stays on track. It's easy to get heated so try to keep your emotions in check.

- "This is hard for me to talk about. Try not to take things personally if I say things the wrong way."

- "You've stated it as if I am the main problem. But it goes both ways. Each of us needs to be willing to make some changes in this area."
- "The more I push for sex, the more you resist. The more you resist, the more frustrated and impatient I get. Can we find some middle ground?"
- "How about we come up with three or four things we're willing to do differently that might help us make some headway on this?"

If the man is having difficulty maintaining an erection, a woman's first reaction should be to say nothing and take his lead. He might focus on other aspects of sex play until his erection returns. If he is obviously distressed or wants to end lovemaking abruptly, avoid the cliché "This happens to all men eventually." These comments might help.

- "There are many times I'm not easily aroused during sex. I just expect those things to happen and am not bothered by it at all."
- "Here, do this (find a pleasing alternative). I love it when you do that."
- "Stay here beside me. I'd really love a massage right now." (It's helpful for the man to remain in the situation and find some other sensual activity to perform. Distraction plus the passing of time is often all it takes for the erection to return.)

If your husband experiences arousal difficulty but approaches you later on for sex, it's helpful to go along. He may want to prove to himself that his problem was a temporary glitch. If you turn him down, he may wonder if you did so because of his most recent performance.

Sample Script

"We need to talk"

Laurie and Tim have been married for twelve years and have two children. Both work outside the home but Laurie has late afternoons available to get the kids off the school bus. Their sex life has become a source of tension over five years. Tim thinks Laurie is not interested in sex as much as she should be—she rarely initiates sex—and Laurie thinks Tim places far too much emphasis on having sex. Tim believes he has tried everything to fix the problem. He has been tolerant and has gone for weeks sometimes without approaching Laurie sexually. When he finally does approach her he has little patience if she is not in the mood. Laurie views her sexual desire as connected to her feelings about Tim. When she feels taken for granted or ignored, her desire for him goes out the door. In the past they've talked about this issue only for brief moments and never delved into it.

TIM: (Shortly after making love.) That was nice. I'm hoping we can do this more often.

LAURIE: Do you have to bring that up now?

TIM: I think we need to talk about it. We've been bothered by it for a long time.

(Tim resisted getting annoyed when Laurie got defensive.)

TIM: I don't expect us to always be in agreement about this. But whatever we've tried to do about it so far hasn't worked.

LAURIE: I've told you what I think. We just have different levels of desire and the only time you seem to care about our relationship is when you haven't had enough sex.

TIM: That's not true.

LAURIE: The fact that you think that is part of the problem.

(Right now they are in a standoff. Tim is feeling unfairly blamed and Laurie doesn't see his side. If they are not careful, each could view the other as uncooperative and once again the issue will be re-shelved.)

TIM: You're right that I get sidetracked by my job and I'm not always in a great mood when I get home. And we haven't had a night out in a while.

(He is finding merit in her point of view. That's good.)

TIM: But in all honesty, if I make changes in those things I still think you won't be as interested in sex.

LAURIE: Well that might not be the only reason we don't have sex as often as you'd like. Maybe we have different drives.

TIM: All I'm saying is that I'm willing to try to do something different so we can both be more satisfied.

LAURIE: Okay, but I'm not sure what to do differently. I can't just start having sex more often. I'd feel like a phony.

TIM: I'd really like it if you initiated it. Then I'd know you are interested. That way, if you don't want to have sex one day I can still believe you haven't lost your interest overall. And I'd like you to be more playful when we're not having sex.

LAURIE: Playful?

TIM: You know, like we did when we were dating; more affectionate, more teasing. You always gave me the impression you desired me.

LAURIE: But if I do that, you'll just run with it and think I'm always interested in having sex. I don't want to lead you on.

TIM: Be playful anyway! I just want us to have more fun and not be so uptight. If we can have sex a little more often than we have been, I can live with that. But I need to think you are still attracted to me and want me.

LAURIE: And I need to think you care more about me than just how often you get laid.

TIM: Back to that again.

LAURIE: Yes. It's crucial. We don't ever sit down and talk or do things together. We're both tired and stressed. You don't even watch a DVD with me. You're always on the computer.

TIM: I promise I will pay a lot more attention to you. But at some point I'd like you to initiate sex and be willing to make love a little more than you do now. Does that seem fair?

LAURIE: I don't know, but we can give it a try. Don't expect a complete turnaround overnight.

TIM: I won't. Let's do our best and see what happens.

This issue tends to recycle and couples faced with it must expect ups and downs. No solution will work perfectly all the time. As long as the marriage is reasonably sound and communication is open, mismatched sexual desire is manageable and need not interfere with overall couple satisfaction.

Chapter Seven

Parenting

MARLENE'S DAUGHTER JENNIFER was still chatting online with her friends when she was supposed to be helping her mother unload groceries from the car.

"In a minute," Jennifer kept saying.

"I don't have a minute," Marlene said.

Just then Marlene's husband Ron came downstairs. Marlene asked him, "Would you tell her to get off the computer *now!*"

Then Marlene heard Jenn stomping up the stairs to her bedroom, obviously furious at her father.

"Now what happened?" Marlene said.

"I told her to get off the computer. She didn't do it immediately so I unplugged it," Ron said. "She yelled at me so I told her to go to her room and forget about going to the movies tonight with her friends."

Marlene was exasperated. "I ask you for help and you go and make the situation worse!"

Effective coparenting isn't always easy. It's especially difficult when the parents don't agree on how to discipline the children.

Discipline Dilemmas and "Emotional Soup"

In order for a couple to effectively communicate about child-rearing, child-rearing must be the main topic being discussed. That may seem obvious, but couples who repeatedly disagree about parenting styles are no longer communicating about parenting—they just think they are. Couples who struggle with ongoing parenting hassles are juggling many issues. I call those issues "emotional soup" and there are many, like the following:

1. If a child continues to misbehave or have problems that parents cannot deal with, parents worry about their own adequacy as parents. That creates anxiety, and anxiety sometimes interferes with judgment.

2. Since parents rarely are in 100-percent agreement all the time about parenting, differences of opinion can widen when problems with raising children persist. The more "strict" parent will blame the more "lenient" parent, and vice versa.

3. If one parent is more involved with the children on a daily basis, he or she may pull rank, further creating division. Similarly, if one parent is underinvolved with the kids on a regular basis (perhaps due to job demands), he or she may want to get their way with a parenting issue as a way to feel involved and influential.

4. There may be separate marital problems that become exposed or inflamed when the parents are trying to be effective coparents. For example, if one spouse feels neglected in the marriage, he or she might object when the spouse is perceived as neglecting one of the kids (or there might be an objection if the spouse is viewed as being too involved with the kids at the expense of quality couple time).

5. Today, more kids than not live in a "nontraditional" home. Stepparents have a particularly difficult role. They are expected to take on responsibility for their stepchildren (buy them things, perhaps provide a home, take them places, help with homework and other needs) but often possess less power than the biological parent does. The biological parent typically feels a bit guilty for having put their child through a divorce and is therefore uncomfortable when the stepparent and stepchild are at odds.

6. Each parent has his or her own upbringing to deal with. One may want to repeat many of the parenting styles his or her parents had while the other may want to do it completely differently from the way he or she was raised.

So let's imagine that twelve-year-old Jimmy is receiving poor progress reports in school—mostly for failure to hand in his homework on time. Mom and Dad are concerned and discuss the problem. How well or how poorly they communicate depends upon how much "emotional soup" they are wading into. If they are open-minded and flexible with no marital resentments and no major childhood issues, they will come up with a plan and implement it. Then they will follow up to see if their plan needs revising or not. Case closed. But this is rarely the case.

Imagine that one of them has this parenting philosophy: "My parents cracked the whip hard and I didn't turn out bad." And imagine that the other parent prefers a more gentle approach. Now they are wading into emotional soup, trying to discuss the best way to get Jimmy to do his homework when in reality other emotional issues are driving the conversation (for instance, whose parents were more effective; whose current parenting style is better). Unless they have a conversation about their overall difference in parenting style, any future conversation about any parenting topic will get bogged down by that underlying issue. (The SAIL approach to communication that was discussed in Chapter 2 is required reading for couples who get stuck in a tug-of-war over parenting.)

Ineffective conversations in that regard would show one trying to persuade the other to go along with his or her views. It would turn a discussion into a debate, then an argument—and no matter who "wins," the couples loses. An effective conversation would involve a mutual effort to see the importance of each other's ideas and come up with a strategy they are willing to try even if they don't fully agree. One of my favorite phrases I tell couples over and over who are in a competitive tug-of-war with each other over some

Conversation Peace

Stepparents have a special role in a child's life, a role that is also very challenging. Some of the complications of effective stepparenting can be avoided if certain guidelines are followed. First, it's helpful for the stepparent to spend one-on-one time with each of the kids. Getting to know each child better can create goodwill. Stepparents must have a say in determining household rules but should not be heavy-handed in enforcing the rules. When possible, the biological parent should be the enforcer. Family meetings are a good way to handle family problems. Finally, the stepparent should explore with the kids how they would like to refer to the stepparent.

issue: There is no love at the competitive level. At the competitive level, winning and being "right" outweigh the greater goal of being a team with mutual respect and give and take.

What's the Real Problem?

The most commonly stated reason couples see a marriage therapist is for "communication" problems. To the couple, a communication problem represents a skill deficit. If only they could say the right words, not interrupt, listen, and keep the volume down to an acceptable level, they'd be fine. To an experienced therapist, a communication problem usually means that the issues being discussed are not the only issues driving the emotional responses during the conversation. The less aware you are of the underlying emotional factors that are affecting your judgment of the situation, the less effective you will be in parenting (and in talking with your spouse about the best way to parent). Also, the more emotional soup you are in, the less effective you will be at listening—and without listening, communication is lost.

So, how can you tell if the parenting issue you and your spouse are trying to discuss is really only about parenting and not influenced by some other issue? Unless one or both of you is very insightful, you'll need to look for certain clues.

- The parenting problem does not seem to improve over time, despite commonsense approaches to dealing with it.
- Talking about a parenting issue creates ill will between the parents or between a parent and a child.
- As one parenting issue is "solved," another problem crops up quickly.

- When a certain problem makes a parent "see red," some emotional sore spot is being touched.
- When a child problem resembles a marital problem, discussions about how to cope with the child issue can get gridlocked fast. For example, if a woman thinks her spouse takes her for granted and is furious about that, she may overreact with anger at the kids when they take her for granted. If a husband feels his main value to his wife is his paycheck, he may snap at the kids when they ask for money to go to a movie.
- If a parent overidentifies with a child in some way (for example, "He's just like me when I was that age" or "She's a free spirit like I am") then those emotional ties can interfere with judgment.

The more any of those statements seem true for you, the more you are saddled with issues—past or present—that are probably interfering with your ability to communicate and solve parenting issues with your spouse.

How the Past Interferes with Your Present

Think of some memory from your childhood or young adult years that still disturbs you when you recall it. The more intense the disturbance you feel when recalling it, the more likely you will overreact when that memory gets triggered by some present-day incident. If you and your spouse are trying to communicate more effectively about a parenting issue and you seem "stuck," ask yourself if your feelings and opinions, or the current situation you are discussing, remind you of anything from your past. If it does, your job is to separate the past from the present so you can deal with current issues as cleanly as possible. One way is to examine your role in your family growing up. Three common roles are the underfunctioning child, the overfunctioning child, and the do-it-yourself child.

The Underfunctioning Child
This child tends to act more dependent. Others often do for him what he should be able to do for himself. He may or may not have some learning or behavioral deficits. Emotionally, this child expects to be taken care of and expects that others will take responsibility to keep the home functioning well. As an adult, this person may be fine until stressed and then he expects his spouse to take over and manage things. As a result, communication is often problematic because there isn't fairness in the relationship. As a parent, this person may overlook immature behavior on the part of his kids because he is a big kid himself. This person's goal is to take on more responsibilities—even when he doesn't feel it is necessary—in order to bring about fairness within the marriage.

The Overfunctioning Child
This child had many responsibilities growing up and bore them well. Maybe she had to care for younger siblings while Mom worked. Or maybe there were some serious family problems (alcoholism, a disabled parent) and she had to assume a parenting role to her own parents. This child usually does well in school and doesn't want to add to the family's problems by getting in trouble. (However, some are known to act out as they get older, but only if there are more severe problems at home.) This child puts her needs aside for others so easily that she follows the same pattern as an adult. (Many go into teaching or helping professions.) Unless they are married to a

responsible and assertive spouse, this person will usually take over many home and childcare responsibilities and feel overburdened as a result. When communicating to a spouse about parenting issues, it is often to complain that the spouse isn't doing enough or isn't doing things in the right way. This person's goal is to cut back somewhat on feeling and acting so responsible in order to allow the spouse and children to assume more responsibilities—even if they make mistakes.

The Do-It-Yourself Child

This child is similar to the overfunctioning child but in a different way. He or she is less interested in looking out for others and putting aside one's own needs for others. Instead, this person has to fend for himself in life at an earlier age because one or both parents is either physically or psychologically unavailable. Sometimes there is abuse in the home and the child cannot rely on parents for protection. So a ten-year-old boy whose father is rarely around (or whose father is harsh) will learn to fend for himself at school or on the playground and learn by his mistakes rather than by asking Dad for advice. Since expressing feelings was never the way to cope while growing up, they are poor communicators as adults, and they dislike being told what to do. When they have to talk to their spouses about parenting issues, they may come across as stricter or colder, with a "life is rough" philosophy. Many will work hard at their jobs and allow their wives to take on more of the day-to-day disciplining of the children. This person's goal is to be more of an "insider" instead of an "outsider" when it comes to day-to-day family functioning and to learn to see the value in more frequent conversations with their spouse.

Five Ways to Improve Spousal Communication Without Talking

Once you realize that your talks with your spouse about topics such as parenting depend in part on how connected you feel to one another, your communication can improve if your connection to your spouse is enhanced. The following guidelines can help strengthen your marital bond.

1. Minimize how frequently kids sleep in your bed. Yes, it can be fun when young kids jump into bed with Mom and Dad to cuddle. It's understandable when a sick or frightened child might want to sleep with parents. The more often that happens, however, the more the roles of husband and wife start to disappear and the roles of parents begin to take over. Once the husband-wife connection is diminished, couples may argue more about parenting issues when in reality they simply need more quality time together as a couple.

2. Don't reward interruptions by your child when you and your spouse are talking unless it's really urgent.

3. When your children are arguing among themselves, don't automatically rush in to solve the problem for them. Unless someone is at risk for harm, giving kids the opportunity to solve issues themselves (arguments over a toy, for instance) not only helps them learn to take care of themselves, but also helps you. When you don't feel the pressure to always be on top of the situation, you can be less anxious and have more time for yourself or your spouse.

4. Look for ways to carve out time for you and your spouse where your children have to learn to let you be. Depending upon the

child's age, you might insist that "Daddy and I are going to watch this movie by ourselves. I'll check in on you every so often." When at a family restaurant, try to make sure that you as parents sit next to each other as often as possible rather than sitting wherever the kids want you to sit. The idea is to show your children that you and your spouse are a unique unit and deserve time together.

5. Show affection to your spouse in front of the kids. It not only reassures them of your love for one another, it conveys to them that you and your spouse have a relationship apart from being parents together.

Any actions you and your spouse take to promote caring and togetherness will make future conversations about touchy subjects that much easier. Furthermore, couples who are less connected emotionally increase the odds that one of them will be overinvolved with the kids (and perhaps overprotective), which in turn will create conversational roadblocks when the talks are about parenting.

What It Boils Down to Is . . .

When discussing parenting issues, remember that they will never go away. As soon as you think you have parenting figured out, the children get a little older and new issues emerge. It is essential that you develop a communication approach that will help you regardless of the topic at hand. The key attitudes and abilities that will help you immensely are:

A willingness to be influenced by your spouse's ideas and to realize that your opinions are not "truth." You need not always agree but you must be open to ideas your partner has. At a minimum, try to understand and appreciate the motivation and intent behind your spouse's views.

A willingness to de-escalate an escalating argument. This is not the time to feel entitled to get your way. Once an argument is escalating, point out merit in your spouse's views or take back something you shouldn't have said as a way to calm the conversation down.

A willingness to examine your past (especially how your parents treated you) and see if you are overreacting to a current parenting issue because of past influences. So often someone tells me something like "I never wanted to be like my father and yet . . . I'm acting the same way he did." Children who are made to feel inadequate or not very loved growing up often are quick to feel inadequate as parents and respond to children either too harshly or too leniently.

A willingness to admit mistakes and errors in judgment and to admit when a spouse is right or makes good sense. Parenting issues can be tough enough without egos getting in the way.

Good Openings

You should state what you see as the problem or concern and be clear about your desire to do something about it. Comments such as "John's not doing his homework" or "Teenagers who drive have a high accident rate" are incomplete and don't convey what you really want to happen. Harsh accusations and angry tones will only clog up the works.

- "Jeffrey hits his friends when he doesn't get his way. Kids do that sometimes but I'd like us to figure out a way to get him to stop."
- "Our strategy to get Jamie to do her homework isn't working. I'd like to discuss coming up with a new plan."
- "I didn't like the way Mike spoke to you just now. You didn't seem to mind but I thought he was being disrespectful. I'm wondering if we can come up with a consistent way of responding when he talks like that."
- "I've noticed that whenever we discuss discipline, you tend to be more lenient than I'd like and I tend to be stricter. Can we figure out a way to be more on the same page?"
- "Whenever you talk like that to the kids it reminds me of the way my mother used to speak—and that troubles me. I'm not saying you're wrong but I'd like to feel better about it. Can we discuss it?"

Good Follow-Throughs

Once the discussion has begun, don't allow your frustration with the parenting issue to get in the way of speaking respectfully. You're a team. If you don't agree with a viewpoint, say so without sounding critical. Keep your overall goal in mind: to converse effectively enough to agree on a parenting strategy and to feel good about the marital relationship in the process.

- "You're right, I do take a more strict approach with the kids than you do. Let's figure out what's best for this particular problem rather than assume one approach is always better than the other." (Admitting one's own limitations helps keep conversations balanced and productive.)

100

- "Part of our difficulty is that I'm so accustomed to dealing with the kids by myself that I don't always want you to have a say. That isn't fair. Because I'm so involved with the kids I do have a pretty good sense of what works and what doesn't when it comes to discipline. So I'd like you to have a say, but I'd like you to consider my viewpoints, too."

- "I think my problem is that when I hear you raise your voice to the kids, I get upset with you—even when you have a right to be annoyed by them. How about if I try to cut you some slack when you raise your voice, and you try to hold back from yelling when you can?"

- "We always seem to get stuck at the spot where we don't agree on what to do. I have an idea. I want to listen to your viewpoint without challenging it until I can understand why it is so important for you that things get handled your way. Then we'll switch roles."

- "Ordinarily I'd just give in right now and agree to do things your way, but that only makes me resentful and I don't want to do that anymore. We need to come up with a plan that feels fair to both of us."

Sample Script

Sandra and Jon were married eighteen years. Their daughter Michelle was a junior in high school and was in danger of dropping out. Her grades had fallen the past two quarters and she began mouthing off to her parents in a way that wasn't typical. Discussing what to do about Michelle was complicated because Sandra—as many people do when a teenager's behavior seems to be out of control—blamed her spouse somewhat for the situation.

An effective conversation isn't always pretty. Couples will say the wrong things or make matters worse with their tone. Successful couples minimize those errors and get back on track quickly when the conversation gets sticky—and that's what Sandra and Jon show us here.

SANDRA: Michelle is threatening to drop out of school. I won't let her do that.

JON: We may not have a choice.

SANDRA: You give in far too easily with Michelle. I've told you before her behavior is getting out of control and you refused to believe me.

(The discussion is heating up. Sandra opened somewhat harshly. Unless Jon can keep it from escalating, the conversation will get nowhere.)

JON: I didn't refuse. I just had a different opinion. But you're right; the situation's gotten more serious.

(By saying "You're right" Jon helped to de-escalate the conversation.)

SANDRA: Did you speak to her teachers like you said you would?

JON: Not yet.

SANDRA: Why is it everything falls on me to do?

JON: I'll do it. I'll call tomorrow. Sorry.

SANDRA: All right. It's just that it seems to me dealing with Michelle has been my burden and that you've checked out. It's frustrating talking to you when you tell me I'm making a big issue out of nothing. But that's always been our problem with discipline: You stand back and let me handle things alone.

JON: I know. I guess I didn't want to think Michelle was doing anything so out of the ordinary. But I agree with you now that we have to do something. I'm just not sure what.

SANDRA: I say we hire a tutor to help her get her grades back up and restrict where she goes.

JON: I don't know about a tutor. And if we ground her she'll just get more out of control with her anger.

SANDRA: I'm trying to make suggestions and you knock them down.

JON: I'm not knocking them down. I'm just not sure they are the best strategies. Did you notice what just happened? When I do try to get involved with parenting, you get upset with me when I don't agree with you. So I usually back off and let you handle it. Then you complain I've checked out.

SANDRA: (pauses thoughtfully) I hadn't seen that before. But you must admit, over the years you've taken a back seat when it comes to parenting—especially discipline.

JON: I know.

SANDRA: But why? What bothers you about making your voice heard and having to make unpopular decisions with the kids?

(This is a good step. When couples find it hard to budge on some issue or pattern of relating, it's usually because some old fear or wish is being triggered.)

JON: I guess I always thought my dad was too strict and inflexible. I didn't want to be that way.

SANDRA: Okay, that makes sense. But that meant I had to take on a lot of the burden. And sometimes you'd resent me for doing it even though I didn't have much choice. Someone has to be the bad guy once in a while.

JON: Right. That probably wasn't fair.

SANDRA: More than probably. So I understand why you act the way you do, but we have a serious problem with Michelle. I need you to be a part of this. Can you do that?

JON: Yes.

(Now they are on the same page and can start looking at their daughter's problem without being thrown off by their own issues.)

SANDRA: It doesn't mean that we have to handle things my way—I don't even know how best to handle it. I just need us to be on the same team.

JON: I'll call her teachers first thing tomorrow and the guidance counselor, too. I don't know if Michelle is going through a phase or if there's a bigger problem. Do you think she's into drugs?

SANDRA: No idea. I never would have thought so.

JON: And I'd like to talk to Michelle alone first. Okay? Maybe she won't feel ganged up on. Besides, she isn't expecting me to be the one handling this.

SANDRA: All right. It's a start.

(Sandra is willing to be influenced by his suggestions. She doesn't automatically challenge them.)

JON: I don't want her to quit school either. It'd be a huge mistake. We'll figure something out.

Obviously, there is no automatic solution to the problem of a teenager wanting to drop out of school. Parents who can communicate effectively have a better chance of dealing with it than do couples whose communication efforts fall flat.

Chapter Eight

Emotional Distance

COUPLES CAN GO through stretches of time where they feel less connected to one another. Long hours at work, separate interests, humdrum routines, fatigue, and child-rearing can squelch romance and togetherness. For some, this represents the all-too-common rut everybody's heard about. With some dedicated effort, those couples can reignite their romance and feel more emotionally connected.

Are You in a Rut?

Some couples can't climb out of their rut as easily as others and their emotional detachment grows over time. Eventually they become accustomed to the status quo. Reconnecting is absolutely essential. A well-designed study in 1992 by the California Divorce Mediation Project revealed that eighty percent of men and women cited growing apart and losing a sense of closeness as their main reason for getting a divorce. More divorces happen due to emotional detachment than for any other reason.

Usually, each spouse has tried at various times to connect but felt the other was not interested. They were out of synch with each other so that when one pursued closeness the other stayed distant—then they switched roles later. Spouses who feel disconnected must be able to discuss their situation with enough clarity to make sure that they are both trying to connect at the same time and to ensure that one spouse's efforts to get closer won't be ignored by the other.

"We need

How Connected Are You?

1. *If I had to list my spouse's favorite entertainers, books, and foods I'd be fairly accurate.*

   Mostly True____   Somewhat True____   Not Very True____

2. *We don't show a lot of joy or humor but that's okay.*

   Mostly True____   Somewhat True____   Not Very True____

3. *I feel especially proud of my spouse.*

   Mostly True____   Somewhat True____   Not Very True____

4. *We don't show much affection.*

   Mostly True____   Somewhat True____   Not Very True____

5. *I look forward to our time alone together.*

   Mostly True____   Somewhat True____   Not Very True____

6. *If someone asked me what my spouse's hopes and dreams are, I'd have to take a wild guess.*

   Mostly True____   Somewhat True____   Not Very True____

7. *I really enjoy small talk with my spouse.*

Mostly True_____   Somewhat True____   Not Very True____

8. *If I have a personal problem or worry, I'm more likely to figure out what to do by myself.*

Mostly True_____   Somewhat True_____   Not Very True____

9. *My spouse is my close friend.*

Mostly True_____   Somewhat True____   Not Very True____

10. *I wish I could get a divorce.*

Mostly True_____   Somewhat True____   Not Very True____

to talk"

Scoring:

For odd-numbered items, score five points for **Mostly True**, three points for **Somewhat True**, and one point for **Not Very True**. For even-numbered items, score one point for **Mostly True**, three points for **Somewhat True**, and five points for **Not Very True**.

40–50: You feel very connected to your spouse.
30–39: You are connected but could be closer in some areas.
20–29: You are less connected than you should be. Improvement is necessary.
10–19: You are very disconnected. Improvement is essential as your marriage is at risk.

If you responded honestly to this quiz, it provided a reasonable measure of your connectedness to your spouse. Items where you scored only one point tell you the areas that need the most change.

What Makes an Emotionally Distant Couple?

Emotionally distant couples can appear at first glance to be satisfied. They might be good parents together. Neighbors and family might even be surprised if the couple ends up separating or divorced. If they were office mates instead of spouses they might make good coworkers. But passion is greatly lacking. Many of the negative qualities that characterize a very dysfunctional, volatile couple (frequent arguments, lack of respect, ill will) do not often characterize an emotionally distant couple, but they also lack the strong positive qualities that happy couples possess. They don't laugh together. They may not be miserably unhappy but they aren't all that happy, either. At best they might be described as "comfortable," but the word *blah* might be a more accurate description. In severe cases the relationship feels dead.

One tendency of a very emotionally distant couple is that they rarely argue. (That can also be true of some happy couples.) However, while happy couples who don't argue much would claim they have a lot of joy in their relationship, emotionally distant spouses who don't argue lack much positive emotion. Emotionally distant couples don't argue because they simply don't have the energy or the desire to connect. Over time, each spouse has to look at outside interests (friends, hobbies, children, and career) to make them feel more alive. Obviously, there is a greater risk for cultivating a romantic relationship outside of the marriage.

Consider the Consequences

Emotionally distant couples often end up divorced although they may remain together for many years before that happens. Sometimes the divorce is initiated by an affair but on close inspection the affair was really the final nail in the coffin. Sometimes a spouse in such a marriage is surprised that their partner wants a divorce. Since they rarely argued and their life was content, those spouses were blind to the fact that the marriage was dying. The spouse who is taking the initiative to end the marriage will say things like, "I've told you for years I'm unhappy and that we needed to change things, but you wouldn't listen." Sadly, many emotionally distant couples who divorce could have been happier together if they had only made certain changes before it was too late.

Pumping Up the Passion

Emotionally distant couples need to pump up their overall level of intimacy and passion. These couples are sluggish and poorly motivated. When they come to therapy to try to improve intimacy they want their passions stirred without doing what's required to make that happen. They think that they should naturally *feel* closer and if they have to work hard at it to feel that way, well, something must be wrong.

Their situation is not unlike someone who is at a healthy weight in his twenties but over the course of the next fifteen years realizes he has put on an extra twenty pounds. How did that happen? Small changes add up to big changes and the changes can happen gradually so that the person is not fully aware of the ramifications. It's the same way in some marriages. The couple disengages from each other over time but doesn't realize how disconnected they've become until they are entrenched in their new way of relating.

Where to Start?

The first step in making positive changes is viewing your emotional disconnection as similar to a bad habit that has run amok. When you try to stop smoking it feels unnatural not to smoke. When you step on a treadmill after years of not exercising regularly, you will be very sore the next day. When you try to feel closer to the person you married after years of being emotionally distant, it won't feel natural. That doesn't mean change can't happen.

Many people recall the time they first fell in love with their spouse as being an easy thing to do. Everything just fell into place. They didn't have to work at it. Actually, that's not true. Dating someone may not feel like work but the process of falling in love doesn't just happen (infatuations can happen quickly). Dating couples spend time with each other, talk to one another, think of each other when not together, and basically go out of their way to be thoughtful and appreciative. They dream dreams together. They laugh and have fun. If they did none of those things they wouldn't stay together no matter how well suited they might be. Reinvigorating a sluggish marriage takes a similar degree of dedication.

Relearning Intimacy

In my book *The Complete Idiot's Guide to Intimacy* I discuss the four pathways to intimacy: intimacy through talk, touch, togetherness, and thought. Emotionally distant couples are weak in all four areas.

Intimacy Through Talk

Emotionally distant couples don't talk to each other much, and when they do their discussions are brief and fairly shallow. They don't discuss their hopes and dreams or take a strong interest in

"We need
to talk"

Conversation Peace

Couples who lack passion and excitement in their marriage need to do an activity that will make them laugh hysterically or get their hearts pumping. A thrill ride is a terrific way to get hearts beating fast—go to an amusement park, *now!* Find some really fun way to exercise together, or go to a comedy club where you're likely to laugh out loud. Research shows that we feel instantly closer to people when we experience something thrilling with them or when we laugh (not merely chuckle) with them.

what is happening with the other. (Sometimes, one spouse wants more closeness and tries to connect emotionally but is rebuffed.) If they have personal worries or concerns, they are likely to mull them over alone rather than talk about them together. Often, emotionally distant spouses feel lonely but have resigned themselves to the way things are.

Intimacy Through Touch

Emotionally distant couples have a sex life that is infrequent or lacking in passion. It becomes a vicious cycle where a diminished sex life adds to their sense of emotional distance and their emotional distance reduces their desire for a sexual connection. Similarly, nonsexual affection is low. One or both may be quietly angry at the other and not feel like showing affection. Again, one spouse may try to show affection in hopes of rekindling some passion but it usually isn't reciprocated.

Intimacy Through Togetherness

This may be the one area where emotionally distant couples might connect, especially if they have children. Family time involves vacations or day trips or other outings. However, on their own the couple may have separate interests. Many in an emotionally distant marriage often stay late at work to avoid coming home. Doing things together is a natural way to not only have fun, but to chat—so connecting through talking often happens when couples do activities together.

Intimacy Through Thought

Well-connected couples will think positively about each other at times during the day. They look forward to seeing each other. They miss each other. They are fond of one another. Emotionally detached couples do none of those things. If they do think about each other it's in a more negative light.

While it might seem daunting for such a couple to start feeling excitement, love, and passion for each other, the good news is that improvement in one area of intimacy crosses over to other areas so they can gain momentum if they hang in there.

Taking Matters Into Your Own Hands

If any couple needs to start talking to each other it is this couple. However, if they *could* start talking they probably wouldn't be as emotionally distant. Therefore it's important that they try to connect in as many ways as possible in order to feel more connected. These suggestions can get the ball rolling. However, the more disconnected a couple is, the more time it will take to feel a stronger connection.

Have one-sided conversations. The idea is for one person to talk for about ten minutes about any topic (not necessarily the relationship) in which he or she has an interest. The other spouse only speaks up to ask clarifying questions or make supportive comments. To probe more deeply, the questioner can ask things like, "What excites (concerns) you the most about that? Did you have these interests as a child? What would you like to see happen?" The goal is to learn more about a spouse's passions, dreams, or concerns and to share meaningful time together in the process.

Take turns planning something to do together. It needn't be a major production or expensive outing, but each of you should plan some event that the other agrees in advance to go along with. Ideally it would be something you'd both enjoy. Don't let any more than two weeks go by without one planned event happening. Keep doing it until each of you has planned ten activities. This ensures you will be spending enjoyable time together and the planning stage allows for additional time to mull over the other's likes and dislikes.

Increase physical touch and affection. This may seem forced if you and your spouse are very disconnected but it needs to happen. If you associate affection with romance and don't feel romantic, then show affection just as a way to extend caring. Hold hands on occasion, cuddle on the couch, offer a thank-you kiss if the other makes a thoughtful gesture. Agree ahead of time that neither of you will read into the show of affection as meaning anything more than a nice gesture at the time it is offered.

Spend some regular time alone thinking about your spouse's positive qualities. Write them down. What would you miss about your partner if you were not together? What qualities attracted you to your spouse in the first place? What qualities do friends and family appreciate about him or her? Are you proud of your spouse for any reason? Review this list daily. To add a nice touch, tell your partner something from your list every now and then.

Remember that you will be doing activities that you may not feel like doing—and that doesn't mean you are being hypocritical or not true to yourself. If positive feelings of warmth and love for your spouse still exist, they are likely buried under years of neglect. It can take some time to unearth them. Proceed with an open mind and heart and see what happens.

Good Openings

The problem with emotionally distant couples is that they've grown used to having their heads in the sand when it comes to the quality of their relationship. The opening comments to address the issue cannot be tentative, incomplete, or weak. Remember, the spouse on the receiving end either wants to pretend things are fine, isn't motivated to put out much effort, or believes any effort to improve is too little too late. Therefore, your opening remarks must hit hard. Don't make empty threats, but be willing to give genuine ultimatums if need be.

- "I'm very unhappy in our relationship and I want to make things better. But I need your cooperation. Without it, I'm worried about our future together."

- "I've said this before and nothing has changed. It's important that we try to get closer to one another or I don't see myself staying with you. I'm that serious."
- "Maybe you've noticed that we seem to lead parallel lives. I'm not willing to do that anymore. Please let's discuss ways to improve things."
- "I'm not willing to allow our marriage to continue this way. I'm too disconnected from you. I want us to talk now about ways we can bridge the gap. I know you don't think things are that bad but, at least for me, our marriage must improve. Otherwise I doubt we will stay together."

If those comments are met with resistance, be clear that the price to be paid for delaying any effort to make the marriage improve might be the end of the marriage.

Ineffective Openings

- "I'm very unhappy in our marriage. What do you intend to do about it?" (This places control in the other person's hands. It's important to be clear what *you* will and will not put up with.)
- "We're in a rut. We need to spend more time together and have fun." (This invites debate because you are speaking for the both of you. Better to limit comments to how *you* feel and what *you* want.)
- "Do you want to go to a movie this weekend? Let's do something fun together." (These are ineffective because you are dancing around the real issue. State clearly that you are feeling very disconnected and that something needs to be done to correct it.)

Good Follow-Throughs

The follow-through conversation is essential. Emotionally distant couples are good at not keeping the ball rolling in their relationship. At the first sign of conflict or discomfort they back off. When you begin the discussion, don't take the bait if your spouse tries to shrug off your concerns. Your marriage and your future are at stake. Don't be timid.

- "I hear you when you say it's not necessary to make changes. But I cannot stay in this relationship unless I am much happier. I'm willing to work at this. Are you?"
- "I'm going to make plans for us to do things. I understand you may not feel like going anyplace special but I'm making plans anyway."
- "What are two or three things you'd like me to change that you think would make you feel better about us? I promise I will carefully consider what you say and do my best."
- "Two weeks have passed since we agreed to make some changes and we are off-track already. What do you think gets in the way?"
- "I was thinking about all of your good qualities the other day. This is what I came up with. . . ."
- "I know it feels forced that we're trying to spend more time together, but I appreciate your efforts. I don't know how much we'll improve but I'm glad we're trying."
- "We've just started to debate and disagree about what to do. Let's focus on what we are willing to do differently and not get hung up on things we disagree about."

Ineffective Follow-Throughs

Anything that forces a no-win debate or keeps you from making gains in your effort to reconnect must be avoided during conversations.

- "Well if you're not going to keep trying, why should I?" (If all it takes is one of you to stop trying for you both to stop, you won't make headway.)
- "You're the one who's never interested in having sex." (No blaming. Each of you must look at the bigger picture and admit how you failed to emotionally connect when you could have.)
- "Maybe we're not meant to be together." (That may or may not be true. Your decision now is to move forward or to forget about moving forward. Which is it?)
- "Other couples don't have these problems." (What are you willing to agree to do that might make the situation improve?)

More Follow-Throughs

Spouses who feel disconnected often have mixed feelings about getting closer. They're not ready to end a marriage but one or both seem unwilling to really put forth the effort needed to make the marriage thrive. Conversations about making improvements therefore can be unproductive. Further, those conversations sometimes stir up old resentments, which can make more dialogue seem too taxing. The goal is not to point fingers or dredge up everything that's problematic but to agree to go one step at a time—making small gains—until optimism and goodwill replace pessimism and indifference.

- "Please bear with me. I'd like to see if things can improve but my heart isn't in this yet."
- "You're right that I've ignored many of your attempts to get closer. However, I can recall times when I felt neglected by you, too. This isn't about who's more to blame. Let's figure out one thing we can agree to do that might help us feel more connected and start there."
- "Sometimes I want to get closer and sometimes I don't. That's frustrating for both of us. But I understand we need to go in one direction consistently, otherwise we'll just continue to flounder."
- "That's a good idea to help us feel more connected. But I know my heart isn't in this. Please understand that I will do this but I won't necessarily feel closer to you just yet. It's the best I can do for now."

Sample Script

"We need to talk"

Erin and Luke are in an emotionally distant relationship. They have children and Erin doesn't want to upset their lives by leaving Luke. She cares for him, maybe even loves him, but she's no longer sure she is "in love" with him. She's begun looking at other men and wonders what it would be like being married to them. Finally, Erin decides it's essential to address her concerns but doubts anything will work. The couple's ultimate goal is to come up with a plan they both agree to that holds some promise to improve their sense of emotional connection.

ERIN: I can't pretend I'm happy anymore. I'm not happy in this marriage.

LUKE: Our marriage isn't bad.

ERIN: It's not good. When was the last time we held hands or looked forward to making love? We rarely kiss. When we do it's going through the motions. We've lost the romance.

LUKE: It's not like I haven't tried.

ERIN: When? It seems like every time I want us to go out together you aren't interested.

(The blame-game has begun. It's necessary to get away from that.)

LUKE: The other night I opened a bottle of wine, wanted to watch a movie, asked if you wanted to watch it. You had a sip of wine and were fidgety the entire time, like you wanted to be anywhere else.

ERIN: You're right, that did show effort on your part. And I wasn't that interested because I'd felt let down by you many times before. I'm not blaming you. We're both responsible. But the fact remains if we didn't have children I don't think I'd want to stay married.

LUKE: Don't let the kids hear you say that.

ERIN: Do you feel that way, too? Honestly?

LUKE: No. Things aren't that bad, but they could be better.

ERIN: Please, tell me what needs to happen to make them better.

LUKE: Well, for starters you could act like you're happy to see me when I get home from work. You're always busy with the kids or on the computer.

ERIN: Yes, I am.

(Good. No defensiveness.)

LUKE: We hardly ever have sex.

ERIN: And why is that?

LUKE: But I'm not sure I'm all that interested now, anyway.

ERIN: So neither of us is that interested. That makes it hard to make improvements.

LUKE: Why would I be interested in someone who rejects me all the time?

(A very loaded statement. He's blaming Erin, but she doesn't take the bait.)

ERIN: I have rejected you. But if we're both honest, I've felt rejected, too. We do it to each other. So when you finally show interest in me I'm not willing to be all that enthusiastic.

LUKE: Same here.

ERIN: So we're back to the real question: Do we want to make improvements or not? And if so, what should we do?

LUKE: I'm not sure how I feel; not sure what I want anymore. Maybe talk more or do more things together.

ERIN: Sounds promising but when I try to talk to you, you ignore me.

LUKE: You always complain about something.

ERIN: So we should talk about things that aren't complaints. Okay, I'll do that. Tell me now, just off the top of your head, what is your fantasy wife like?

LUKE: Huh?

ERIN: Your dream-come-true wife. Tell me about her. I promise I won't take offense.

(This is an excellent strategy if no one gets defensive.)

LUKE: (smiling) She speaks with a French accent. **(Humor is good at this point.)** I guess I'd be her one and only. She'd have time for me; I wouldn't come in last place at the end of the day. If I didn't want to talk about something, she'd understand and accept that. We'd have fun together, go places and do things. Sex wouldn't be an issue. It would happen naturally—and often. So tell me about your dream-come-true guy.

ERIN: I like your dream wife, by the way. She sounds like she's having fun and that she loves you very much. My dream husband would always be thoughtful. He'd always see how his smallest action affected me and would make sure he never did anything that was annoying or thoughtless. And he'd want me for me, not just for my body. He'd enjoy showing affection, wouldn't be embarrassed about it in public. Sex, at least some of the time, would be romantic—candles, wine, things like that. He wouldn't just roll over and start groping. When I walked into a room his eyes would light up. A day would never go by where I doubted his love for me.

LUKE: We have a lot of work to do.

ERIN: Yes. And once we agree to a plan we have to stick with it. So maybe we should check in once a week and talk about how we're doing, if we're making progress or not.

LUKE: What if we try and nothing happens?

ERIN: You mean what if it's too little too late? It's nice to know that concerns you.

LUKE: What I mean is, I'm not sure my motivation is that strong. I'm willing to try.

ERIN: Maybe we should stick to a plan and not give up at least for a few months. Just keep at it. If we stop, we may not make it. Are you willing to stick with a plan no matter if it feels like it might be a waste of time?

LUKE: Maybe.

ERIN: Unless we can commit to this, it absolutely will fail. And we will fail.

LUKE: Okay. Let's get specific about what we each need to do differently, work on making changes, and touch base once a week to see if we're on track or not.

ERIN: It's a deal.

There is hope if you stay on track. The more you try and fail, the more discouraged you will be.

"We need to talk"

Chapter Nine

Money and Chores

WHEN A COUPLE tells me "We don't communicate" and I do some probing, I usually discover that what they don't communicate well about are financial matters and the distribution of chores (parenting, sex, and outside interests round out the top five divisive issues).

It's a mistake to believe that arguments about money would disappear if you had a lot more of it. Even millionaires argue about spending. In some regards, the way a couple deals with issues about spending can reveal their capacity for showing love. A mature level of giving and receiving, of looking at things from the other's viewpoint, and trying to balance both spouses' needs are important qualities when dealing with issues of love and money.

Similarly, a mature couple doesn't simply draw a line in the sand and share all chores fifty-fifty. Instead, they make a more careful consideration of what is most fair given all of the other demands and responsibilities in their lives.

House Rules

Every household has a set of rules—usually unwritten—that members tend to follow or fight about. The main rules have to do with spending and house-related chores. Each spouse has a set of expectations and when those expectations are not met ("You didn't clean up your mess. . . . You spent *how much* at the store?") tensions mount. Money and chores are hot spots for couples for three reasons.

1. They represent ongoing issues that can never be solved once and for all. No agreement they come up with can always apply. That's because a couple's situation changes over time depending on income, the presence of children, health status, the economy, emergencies, and so forth.
2. They represent possible differences in personality. Some people are savers by nature, others like to spend money more freely. Similarly, some people are "neat freaks" who can't sit still if a home is untidy while others are at ease living in clutter and a little grime. Some people are just plain lazy while others are busy beavers.
3. They represent differences in values. One spouse yearns to buy a motorcycle while the other believes the money is better spent on a swimming pool. One would rather spend a free Saturday doing something fun, while the other thinks it's important to catch up on yard work and save the fun for later.

A common mistake couples make when they debate these issues is that they presume they can come up with a permanent solution to these concerns when, in fact, no permanent solution exists that will make each side happy. It's a lucky couple who shares very similar beliefs about chores and spending, but most couples differ enough to cause occasional resentments or arguments.

The Issues Behind the Issue

Chapter 2 addressed the fact couples sometimes argue about issues that are not about the topic being discussed. The emotion that is fueling the disagreement often has roots elsewhere. So a couple who argues about vacuuming floors and raking leaves are probably arguing about overall *fairness* in the relationship. If one spouse feels strongly that the relationship is unfair, surface arguments may get nowhere until the underlying issue is addressed fully.

For example, Maria's husband Larry was huffing and puffing, trying to remove hard snow-packed ice from their driveway. He asked Maria for some assistance and she refused. He got annoyed because their driveway was slippery and she needed to be able to drive her car as much as he needed to drive his. Maria felt for a long time that Larry didn't help her with certain household chores when she asked—in fact, he made as much of a mess as the kids did. And while he was allowed to spend money on whatever he wanted, she had to check in with him first when she wanted to buy something out of the ordinary. "It's not about the snow," she said later. "It's about fairness."

A fairness issue is also a control issue. If one spouse feels the other is unfair, he or she also thinks that the spouse has too much control.

The Issue of Money

Money—how much is available and how much is spent—taps into deeper issues for many people. If you and your spouse argue frequently about spending (how much to spend and who decides) look more closely at possible underlying issues. For example:

Talk Alert

If a spouse is controlling in many areas (not just financial) such as trying to control who you socialize with, who your friends are, what you do in your free time, who you are calling on your phone, what you wear to work, how much time you spend with your parents or family, and so forth, you are living with someone with a personality disorder who is jealous and insecure. See a discussion about this in Chapter 3.

Fear of loss of security. Some people worry about being poor or not having enough money for retirement and therefore become dictatorial about spending. While such concerns are reasonable, they can *always* be used as justification for not spending—after all, "You never know what the future will hold and it's better to be safe than sorry!" Unless there is some give and take, money will always be a sore spot and possibly a cause of deep resentment.

Fear of loss of self-esteem. For some, spending money to keep up with the neighbors or spending money on luxury items can be done to boost weak self-esteem. If you are concerned more about what others will think of you and worry about impressing others, your spending habits won't always be wise.

A need to feel good. Some people spend money they shouldn't for the immediate gratification they feel. "Shopaholics" spend money wastefully and repeatedly because it offers them a feeling of comfort or a release from tension. Some need to have "mad money" on hand, otherwise they feel too constrained.

To regulate intimacy. Some people would rather buy gifts for a spouse as a way to say "I love you" because they feel uncomfortable showing love in other ways. Some will purchase items as a way to "get back" at a spouse, or will control the purse strings because of resentment over other marital problems.

If one spouse has more say over spending, the other (typically) has more say over sex. What's really happening is an effort to balance power. It isn't always a conscious decision on a person's part to withhold sex as a way to protest a spouse's control over finances.

"We need to talk"

Conversation Peace

Money issues can be especially problematic in remarriages. Often, one spouse comes into the new marriage with some kind of financial settlement and it can be hard to sort out what money should be used for what purpose. These general guidelines help for most marriages and remarriages:

- Money acquired before the marriage belongs to that person.
- Inherited money belongs to that person who inherited it.
- Money acquired during the marriage belongs to both spouses.
- Unless otherwise negotiated, children are the financial responsibility of the biological parents

---

People can lose their sex drive when they feel unhappy or develop performance problems when they feel under their spouse's thumb financially.

The Issue of Chores

Since most married couples today are dual-earners, chores—who does them and how often—is a thorn in the couple's side. The issue is especially troublesome when one spouse was not working outside the home—or was working part-time—and now is working full-time. Another situation where this becomes a problem is when a full-time worker stays home to raise a child. Now each spouse's expectations can be very different from one another and problems can arise that never existed before (and if income is reduced, money can become an issue). Again, the overriding issue is fairness. Unless each spouse feels that the distribution of chores is fair—given their unique circumstances—resentments will build.

At the highest level of maturity, money matters and chores will be handled well by a couple. Neither spouse will be reckless in spending nor hoard money. Disagreements about spending based upon one's preferences and values will be expected and there will be a thoughtful amount of give and take. Chores may be assigned or not but there will be agreement on what needs to be done and how often and allowances will be made when life events interfere. If one spouse says "I'll get around to it" he or she means it. The hallmark of the successful couple is flexibility. The more stuck they are to maintain a certain role—"I'll mow the lawn, you do the laundry"—the more complicated life can become if one spouse can't perform the necessary task.

The less mature the couple, the more they will cling to "rules" that are really just their own preferences and will make the other person wrong if things aren't done a certain way.

A good guideline is for each spouse to be well aware of the checkbook balance, the usual monthly income and expenses, and amount of money in savings or investments. Otherwise, the uninformed spouse may have unrealistic financial expectations.

Going to Extremes

How a spouse feels about spending and chores can tell you a lot about his or her personality and what to expect during discussions. When it comes to money, broadly speaking, one is more of a spender or a saver. When it comes to doing chores, broadly speaking, one likes things neat and clean or is lazy and untidy. Thus there are four possible combinations when it comes to handling money and chores.

Spender/Neat and Clean: This person enjoys the good life. He or she likes to look good and the house to look good. This is a very active, energetic person. Keeping up appearances is important. He or she may justify spending too much or too frivolously because a lot of time is spent keeping the house and yard beautiful. Any marital dissatisfaction will be offset by spending money on pleasurable things—which in turn may create more marital problems. Disagreements with this spouse about chores and spending are likely to reflect value differences.

Spender/Untidy and Lazy: This person has a sense of entitlement. Life is to be lived fully and to heck with the day-to-day responsibilities. Early in a marriage, this person can be extremely fun (if money is available) since all he or she wants to do is play. Over time this person comes across as immature and irresponsible. Unless each spouse is this way (unlikely) this person's partner will be the more responsible one and feel burdened and overwhelmed. Ironically, the spender/untidy person tends to be attracted to those who might be less carefree since they need someone to reel them in and put on the brakes, but they will argue with that person for doing so. Spousal disagreements in this case sound like a harried parent lecturing an irresponsible child.

Saver/Neat and Clean: This person is super-responsible but uptight. He or she doesn't know how to have fun. It's all business with this person. Usually they are very logical—almost to a fault. They can justify living a spartan existence and an orderly life and cannot relax unless things are in their place. Emotionally they are a bit repressed. Whatever emotional hurts or losses they experience they try to cover up. They don't wear their feelings on their sleeve and are impatient with overly emotional dramatic people. They have a "stiff upper lip" philosophy and have a hard time showing tenderness. Ironically, they tend to be attracted to people who are warm and carefree and then find themselves at odds with them. They do this because they need to have more warmth and animation in their lives, but feel unable to bring it about themselves. Disagreements with this person about chores or money tend to wind up as debates. They like to lecture and they think they know best. This person's goal is to loosen up and to realize that marriage isn't just about following a set of daily rules. It's about giving, having some fun, and friendship.

Saver/Untidy and Lazy: This person can be controlling and wants to be attended to. He or she may work very hard, not want to spend money, and expect to come home and be taken care of. If he earns more money than his spouse, he expects her to do the housecleaning. This is a very traditional mentality that only works best with someone who also possesses a traditional view of relationships. If this is a woman, her husband is also a hard worker but who is willing to take on household chores readily. He likely has an easygoing personality and is not one to stir up conflict. The saver/untidy person doesn't consider himself to be lazy. He or she simply has less of an interest spending energy on housework. But since housework must get done, it can be unfair to the other spouse. Hiring a maid would be ideal, but this person won't spend the money.

Putting Limits on Money

Should all the money be in one pot and accessible to each spouse? Should the couple have separate accounts, split the bills, and spend whatever they want for themselves according to what's in their own account? Should the one who is more of an expert in finances make the final decision about any expense?

All three methods can work fabulously and fail miserably. It's not the "rule" that makes the situation work, but the attitude and character of the people setting up the rule. For example, I've worked with couples who keep all money accessible to one another in joint accounts. With some of those couples, there was mutual trust, goodwill, and fairness so that strategy worked. Yet another couple did the exact same thing but for a different reason. The wife didn't trust her husband to have a separate account—she wanted to know what he was spending money on at all times. This "rule" about a joint account led to many arguments but the real problem was lack of trust, not a faulty rule.

Similarly, I've worked with couples who had separate bank accounts and they split all bills including vacation costs. Some did this because each one felt the other was either too stingy or too reckless with money when it was in a joint account and accessible to both. In these cases, their rule about having separate accounts was necessary to limit the ill will that came about due to trust issues.

Bottom Line

Rules work best—whether they are rules about spending or rules about chores—when they add clarity to what is expected and help organize a couple's life. If a great deal of yard work and housework needs to get done before the big family reunion barbecue, it makes it easier to plan your time when you already know what is expected of you. While there are many couples whose problems with spending or chores stem from bigger problems such as immaturity, an inability to be trusted, or a domineering personality, the typical couple who argues about spending or chores does so because of personal preferences and values. What's important to one spouse (for instance, a shiny clean house or a savings account that cannot fall below a certain dollar amount) may not be as important to the other. Then it takes an ability to communicate effectively in order to achieve some happy medium.

Good Openings

If you have a history of disagreeing about spending, you will probably *always* disagree to some extent. Conversations about spending can't fix those differences but can help manage them—if you are prepared to talk about money periodically without getting aggravated.

- "I know I spend money more freely than you do. And I understand the value of saving more—which is what you want. But I want you to understand that I do hold back from buying many things, and the things I do buy make life a little happier. I value that as much as you value saving."
- "I know I can be a pain when I don't want to spend any money and that you have a right to spend on things that make our life happier. But I wish you'd lean more in my direction sometimes. The more I see you appreciating my point of view, the easier it is for me to not hassle you about spending."
- "It's frustrating that we don't see eye to eye on spending. I don't want to argue every time a spending issue comes up. Somehow I need to show you I can curtail spending so you can trust my judgment, and I need to see you be more flexible about spending so I don't feel so stressed whenever I spend money."
- "I'm wondering if we can agree on a certain amount of money to save each month. That way we both win. I can spend more freely as long as we are saving, and you'll have some peace of mind knowing that money is being put away each month."
- "We've debated the issue many times. We each know how the other thinks and feels. We just disagree about how to spend money. But we love each other and have to live with each other. So we need to find a way to accept these differences and argue less."

Similarly, discussions about chores will likely be repetitive. There is no once-and-for-all solution since any agreement can be ineffective once kids come along or there are changes in work hours or health status.

- "The situation with housework doesn't feel fair to me and I'm starting to resent it. I'd like to talk about ways to make it fairer."
- "It seems that when we agree on chores, you can count on me to do what I said I'd do. But too often I can't count on you to follow through on your end. That frustrates me. Is there something I don't understand from your point of view?"
- "This is always a touchy subject for us. How can I talk about it so that you will find it helpful?"
- "I don't think it's fair the way we do chores. I'm wondering what percentage of chores you think is fair for you to do?"
- "Now that I'm working more hours, we need to find a fairer way to divvy up the chores."

Good Follow-Throughs

A failure to follow through is a surefire way to keep resentments burning. Difficult conversations are difficult precisely because the topic raises anxiety and anxiety causes many dialogue mishaps. Plodding through those mishaps and trying to get back on track can help you arrive at some kind of satisfying conclusion—for now.

- "I'm sorry I'm being argumentative. That never gets us anywhere. But since we will disagree about spending in the future, we need to find some middle ground or find a way to give in to the other without resenting it."
- "Ordinarily one of us ends the conversation right about now. I'm glad we're hanging in there."

- "We often try to make each other wrong about spending. You're not wrong for wanting to spend more than I do, and I'm not wrong for wanting to spend less. We just think differently. Still, how do you want to handle the situation this time? It won't be long before we face the same situation again."
- "How about if you tell me what makes sense about my viewpoint, and I'll tell you what makes sense about yours. Then we need to come to an agreement about what to do this time around. We might choose differently next time."
- "Thanks for trying to find some middle ground."

Follow-Throughs Regarding Chores

- "I know housework isn't fun but it needs to get done. It isn't fair that we both get the benefits of a clean house but only one of us does most of the work."
- "You keep telling me that you do help out and that I overlook what you do. That might be true. I guess we have a different set of expectations about what needs doing."
- "We're both busy and we're both tired when we get home. Maybe there are some chores we can do less often. What are your thoughts?"
- "When you don't do the chores that need doing and you leave them up to me to do, I begin to think you're angry at me for something. Is that true?"
- "Every time you roll your eyes I feel like ending the conversation. But the truth is we need to come up with some way to deal with this issue, otherwise we'll just keep resenting each other."

Sample Script

The following script is about the issue of chores but in many ways the same words could be used discussing money. Dawn feels overburdened by housework. Getting Matt to help out is like moving a large boulder—a lot of effort to make a little progress. If she just didn't bother asking him and did the work herself, things would get done faster, but she'd resent it. This is how she approached her latest conversation.

DAWN: It seems like every day I spend my free time getting caught up on housework. I need your help more than I've been getting it.

MATT: You don't know how to relax.

DAWN: That might be true.

(Good. Better to admit that than get argumentative.)

DAWN: But if I relaxed as much as you do, very little would get done. I'm asking if you can do more chores on a regular basis—something I can count on—so I don't have to do as much as I'm doing now.

MATT: I'm tired when I get home.

DAWN: Me too. I'm not saying we can't relax when we get home from work. I'm saying that certain chores must get done regularly and it seems to me that I end up doing them.

MATT: Okay, tell me what to do and I'll do it.

DAWN: That doesn't really help.

MATT: Why not?

DAWN: I appreciate your offer but you're making me in charge. It's not about you doing what I ask. I need you to be able to notice what chores need doing so I don't always have to ask. I'm tired of being the one in charge.

MATT: I just offered to help and it isn't good enough. Sometimes when I do help out you criticize what I did. So I think "why bother?"

DAWN: I didn't realize I was being critical.

MATT: You are.

DAWN: Okay, I'll work on that. Let me know the next time you think I'm too critical. But my main point is I want you to notice if something needs to be cleaned or picked up off the floor and just do it.

(Good. She didn't debate him and she didn't get sidetracked.)

DAWN: Don't wait for me to point it out. It doesn't take long to sweep the kitchen floor or pick up the kids' toys.

MATT: But maybe I see something needs cleaning and I intend to get around to it but I don't do it when you think I should. Then you think I'm not willing to help.

DAWN: That is a problem. Sometimes I leave dishes unwashed thinking you will get to them but they're still there the next day. It makes me think you really don't intend to wash them after all.

MATT: But I will. Just give me time.

DAWN: But if I give you time and it isn't happening, I get angry. If I speak up, I feel like a nag. I think we need to come to some agreement on what chores get done, who does them, and how soon.

MATT: You think too much. This is getting too complicated.

DAWN: This is where I get stuck in our conversation. You say you're willing to help but you're also telling me you want me to assign chores to you and that you should have the freedom to do them whenever you want and I shouldn't nag.

(Good. Instead of getting defensive, she clarifies her understanding of what's being said.)

MATT: I don't think I'm saying that. I'm saying it frustrates me when you don't give me a chance to do what needs doing on my own schedule.

DAWN: Okay, let's try to understand the spirit of what each of us wants. The spirit of what I'm saying is that more chores get done by me than by you. And when I wait to give you time to do some chores, sometimes the wait is very long. What I'd like is to be able to rely on you to do some things more regularly—without my having to ask—and in a timely fashion. Is that something you can do?

MATT: I suppose so. Like what kind of things?

DAWN: We have to sort out the details. But usually the carpets need vacuuming at least twice a week. The kitchen floor has dirt and crumbs on it every day. The bathrooms need to be cleaned once a week. Furniture needs to be dusted about once a week. Dishes have to be rinsed before putting them in the dishwasher—not just left in the sink to soak. Coats have to be hung up. That's just the beginning.

MATT: But what about all the things I do that you don't? You don't mow the lawn, I do. You don't get the cars fixed, I do.

DAWN: I realize that. I'm willing to do some chores most of the time by myself. For example, I usually do the laundry and you don't.

MATT: Okay. So let's draw up a list of things we can do on a regular basis. I promise I'll get to these chores more quickly. But cut me some slack if I don't.

DAWN: Sounds good. Nothing can be etched in stone. And if I remind you that something hasn't been done, cut me some slack, too. Don't automatically accuse me of nagging but consider the possibility that you really did let things go too long without attending to them. I just want this to feel fair to both of us.

This conversation is just the beginning. Follow-up conversations should happen soon—to repair any problems with the plan and to monitor progress.

"We need to talk"

Chapter Ten

Online Chatting and Porn

A SPOUSE WHO likes to flirt with others online or who views pornography on a semiregular basis runs a greater risk his or her spouse will eventually consult a divorce attorney. That is the conclusion of countless research studies conducted over the past twenty years. Regular use of pornography weakens marital intimacy, raises the likelihood of infidelity, and increases the odds the marriage will not survive.

The Hardcore Truth

According to Family Safe Media, about 40 million Americans regularly visit porn sites on the web. The majority are online for an hour a week or less. A large minority visit porn sites up to ten hours a week. An hour or less a week may seem insignificant compared to more compulsive users, but it can be enough to weaken a marriage.

Which comes first? Does a less-than-happy marriage cause a spouse to view more sexually explicit material (SEM for short) or does SEM use create a decline in marital dissatisfaction? Studies indicate that use of SEMs seems to bring about a decline in marital satisfaction above and beyond whatever dissatisfaction may have existed before. In other words, viewing of SEMs even occasionally can make very happy marriages less happy, and can make not-so-happy marriages quite unhappy.

There are many reasons why viewing SEMs can cause a decline in marital satisfaction.

- Regular online users of porn eventually regard their spouses as less attractive since they are being compared to people with more attractive bodies. Consequently, regular users of online porn often prefer masturbation for sexual release than sex with a spouse.
- It causes viewers of porn to push for more and more sexual "creativity" from a spouse (veering away from the more common sexual practices), which can result in disagreements, disappointment, and finally a reduction in marital sexual activity.
- Most women whose husbands view porn on a somewhat regular basis feel unimportant, ignored, humiliated, and angry.
- It leads to regular arguments and debates about just how "normal" watching porn is.
- Regular viewing of SEM is addictive. It is associated with less quality family and couple time. Many regular users of online sex sites will wait until their spouse is asleep in bed before going online, further disconnecting themselves from the kind of ritual (going to bed together) that helps maintain marital closeness.
- There is an increased chance of flirting in chat rooms or engaging in sexual activity with an online partner.
- Much viewing of porn is done secretly, without a partner's knowledge. That is because the viewer feels somewhat ashamed

or wants to avoid an argument. Regardless, keeping secrets along these lines puts up walls between spouses and intimacy diminishes.

Excuses, Excuses

If you don't like your husband's use of porn, whether it's X-rated movies accessible with any cable TV subscription, Internet surfing, or the time-tested "centerfold" magazines, your objections might be challenged by him. Your husband is not likely to quickly admit he is wrong. He might or might not be willing to curtail his activities at your request but he is more than likely going to defend them. That is especially true if you challenge him by calling him names ("You're a sex maniac . . . a pervert") or tell him that what he is doing is morally objectionable. He might even tell you that *you're* the one with the problem ("You're a prude . . . you're not with the times . . . you've always had issues with sex"). Below are some of the more common reasons men give to justify their viewing of SEMs—and the myths behind those reasons. (Note: while women may be interested in pornography, men are by far more likely to become addicted.)

"Every Guy Does It. It's Normal."

Every guy doesn't do it. And normal doesn't always mean "healthy." Divorce is normal but far from ideal. Obesity is the statistical norm in this country but is a serious health problem. Most people lie on occasion, but lying is not considered a socially desirable trait. The truth is that viewing porn is associated with greater marital unhappiness and for good reason.

"I'm Not Addicted, So It's Not a Problem."

That's the same argument used by those with alcohol problems who are not "technically" addicted but who nevertheless abuse alcohol. Addiction to Internet porn is a serious problem and wreaks havoc with a person's marriage and life. Like other kinds of addiction, it starts with occasional use and grows from there. The negative impact of porn is not simply due to the amount of time spent viewing, but the effect it has on a spouse and the marital relationship. Rarely does it help a marriage. In small doses it still can damage it.

"You Should Try It—It Can Help Our Own Sex Life."

There is some evidence that people with sexual arousal problems may benefit from watching some kind of sex video as a precursor to having sex with a spouse, but how often that should happen and the long-term benefits are not known. There is evidence that when use of porn creates relationship dissatisfaction, the mutual use of porn slows down the rate of dissatisfaction temporarily—but it fails to reverse the downward trend. In other words, watching porn together is not the answer when porn use is creating problems in a marriage.

"I Can Control It."

Maybe, maybe not. Internet pornography is highly addictive. Internet porn is easily accessible, convenient, affordable (a great deal of pornographic material is free of charge), and anonymous. Regular porn users tell you that looking at the same images becomes boring and novelty is necessary. With just a click users can now access new images instantly, satisfying every sexual desire possible, all from the convenience of home. If he really can control it, then he can drastically cut back.

"If You'd Have Sex More Often, Maybe I Wouldn't Need to Go Online."

Any sort of blaming is a weak excuse. If your spouse is unhappy about your sexual relationship, regular use of pornography is likely to further damage your sex life, not enhance it. If you believe you have a low desire for sex then that issue needs to be addressed honestly. The use of pornography is a separate issue.

"You Never Have Time for Me. . . . You're Always Busy with the Kids."

Again, if there is merit to your spouse's concerns you must honestly do something about them. They still are not reasons to justify porn use.

"You're Sexually Repressed."

If your spouse derives sexual pleasure on a semiregular basis from watching porn, and you have felt ignored or inadequate in the

Conversation Peace

When does viewing pornographic material become an addiction? First, the user develops a tolerance for the images and requires more and more of them in order to bring about the desired effect. Second, addicted users need a "fix" to counteract the withdrawal symptoms they feel when they haven't been viewing pornography. They miss it when it isn't there. Third, other important areas of life (family, social, or career) start to be negatively affected. Fourth, efforts to cut back usually are temporary and inevitably fail.

process, the solution is not for you to accept porn or start viewing it yourself in order to become more sexually liberated. Your spouse is making an excuse. Regular porn viewers show an increased desire for novel, unusual sex acts and might regard a spouse's sexual ways unadventurous or boring by comparison.

Complications from Too Much Porn

To date, research findings are fairly conclusive that regular use of pornography has a debilitating effect on a marriage. Use of online porn (or involvement in some form of online sex) for ten hours a week or more is clearly high-risk behavior and most often associated with a decline in marital stability and an increase in problematic behaviors (mood swings, isolation, interference with job, neglect of other responsibilities, loss of interest in sex with a

Talk Alert

Is it appropriate to install pornography-blocking or monitoring devices on the computer to prevent an addicted spouse from accessing those sites? Yes. In fact, if trust is diminished, you may need to have such a device installed to help with peace of mind. (Obviously a spouse can find computers elsewhere if he really wants to get around this, but a device is still a good idea.) If he objects to those devices and accuses you of mistrusting him or treating him like a child, don't weaken your resolve. He obviously is more concerned about how all of this is affecting him rather than thinking of how it has already affected you. That reveals a lack of insight and sensitivity—and *that* is part of the problem.

spouse, exploring outside sexual relationships, increase in secrecy and deceit, and so on). Watching porn for fewer than ten hours a week is a gray area. For some it represents a high risk that leads to more problems.

For others, their lives still seem manageable. Imagine someone spending five hours a week watching online pornography. There are few couples (especially if they both work and have children) who have five hours a week of quality couple time. Most couples are lucky to have thirty minutes a day. So if someone is spending more time watching pornography than spending quality time with a spouse during the week, a major problem has taken root.

The best advice is simply to avoid viewing hardcore pornographic materials. Never chat online with people in any flirtatious or sexual manner. Below, please find common unhelpful reactions by the spouse of someone who watches porn:

Denial or minimization. Some spouses have a pretty good idea that their partner is regularly watching porn or might be chatting online in some sexually provocative way, but they turn a blind eye.

Believing they don't have the right to object. Very liberal thinkers can get caught up with the idea that they shouldn't object because they don't have the right to tell a spouse what to do. This allows a destructive behavior to go unchallenged.

Fear of being blamed. Some spouses think they must be doing something wrong if their spouse is using pornography. There may in fact be marital issues that need addressing, but the user must be the one to accept responsibility for his actions.

Fear of making matters worse. Ignoring a problem because it might lead to more problems if confronted is a surefire way to make the problem get worse.

Good Openings

Be clear and concise about what you think, how you feel, and what you want. Don't resort to name calling. Don't agree to anything that makes you uneasy. Don't get sidetracked. Anticipate that your spouse might challenge you. If you are unsure how much of a problem this really is or how "normal" it is, consider that viewing pornography on any sort of regular or semiregular basis creates problems and must therefore be drastically reduced or eliminated. Tolerance won't work.

- "I've noticed you're spending time on the computer looking at pornography. You might not think it is a problem but I find it troubling. I'd like to discuss this further."
- "I checked the computer files and noticed that pornographic websites have been accessed on a fairly regular basis. I want to talk with you about that because I'm very disturbed by it."
- "I can understand that looking at naked bodies is very exciting and many people like to view that stuff, but I am uncomfortable with it. I have less respect for you when you do it and I feel turned off sexually to you, as well. We need to talk about this."
- "I've noticed that you stay on the computer late at night after I go to bed. I'm pretty sure you are chatting with someone. I cannot ignore this. I want an explanation. I'm willing to hear the truth. If you tell me everything is completely innocent I have to admit I won't believe you."

- "I've mentioned before that I don't like it when you watch porn. It still bothers me. Something has to change because I know I will feel less love and respect for you if that behavior continues."
- "You've told me before you would cut back or stop and you haven't. I've installed a device to block access to porn sites. I'm not doing this to punish you. I'm doing it so I can start to feel better about you and increase my trust in you."

Good Follow-Throughs

If the spouse who views pornography is genuinely contrite, willing to change, is not addicted, and the marriage is fairly sound, then the discussion will go more smoothly. You still may be upset, hurt, offended, mistrustful, and angry, but chances are very good that all will work out. That is not a typical scenario. Most viewers of pornography—especially if they view it regularly and have been secretive—get defensive. Moving past the defensiveness to the truth and a realistic plan of action is your goal.

- "I hear you getting angry at me for bringing this up. I'm bringing it up because it truly bothers me and I know it has affected our marriage. It certainly has affected how I feel about you."
- "I agree with you that many people find pornography perfectly acceptable, but I don't. And your viewing it does affect me. I feel less attractive to you, less desirable and—let me finish—I feel disrespected. I won't change my views on that. Disrespect in a marriage will kill that marriage."
- "I don't want to get into a debate about how often you go online to view porn. You say it's not that often, I think it's a lot more than that. What I do know for sure is that it is unacceptable to me."

- "I'm not telling you what to do. I'm not controlling you. But you are telling me what to do—to put up with this. You can do what you want, but if you choose to continue to view pornography to the extent you have, I know my feelings for you will change."

- "I'm willing to help you with this. I love you. Maybe it won't be easy for you to stop and I understand that. But I cannot put up with it."

- "I don't want to watch it with you. That won't help me feel better. It will only make me feel worse."

- "You can continue to argue and debate with me but it doesn't change how I feel about your problem. I'm willing to help you with this and we can also work on other areas of our marriage if you are unhappy. But I cannot feel good about you when you continue to watch porn."

Sample Script

"We need to talk"

Alicia had suspicions but no evidence that her spouse, Alex, had a problem with pornography. She mentioned it once before. He denied it and the conversation stopped there. So she waited until she had some hard evidence (data from a computer-monitoring device, e-mails, or catching him off-guard are common methods). Then she went into the discussion with a plan; she was clear about what she wanted to say.

ALICIA: I've noticed that you watch pornography on the computer. At first I minimized it and tried to pretend it didn't bother me. But now I want to discuss it.

ALEX: Sometimes it just shows up and I don't go looking for it. You know how these things go.

ALICIA: I've watched you. And I've checked the computer. You spend a lot of time watching pornography and it isn't by accident. I'm very bothered by it.

ALEX: I can cut back if you want, but really you're making a bigger deal out of it than you need to.

(This is why it was helpful for her to have evidence and be clear about why it bothered her. Otherwise she can be talked out of her concerns.)

ALICIA: This is what I've noticed: You spend less time with me than you used to. We make love less often because you seem less interested. You spend more hours on the computer than ever before. . . .

ALEX: What about all the time you spend on the computer?

(This is an effort to sidestep the problem and focus on you.)

ALICIA: Please let me finish. And you are more irritable. It looks to me like you use pornography as an escape and I worry you can become addicted.

(Wrong approach. She shouldn't psychoanalyze Alex. He might challenge her diagnosis and thereby avoid dealing with the larger issue.)

ALEX: For God's sake I'm not addicted. Who made you a doctor?

(His level of defensiveness is high. Alicia needs to get back on track and talk about what she knows, how she feels, and what she wants.)

ALICIA: Maybe I'm wrong.

(That's helpful. He'll listen better if he thinks you have heard him.)

ALICIA: But the amount of time you spend online watching pornography is too much for me to be happy. It must change. Are you willing to do something about it?

ALEX: Maybe you're looking at things all wrong. Why do I have to change?

ALICIA: Please hear me. I'm not saying you are bad or terrible or anything like that. I am saying that the amount of time you spend watching porn has made me more angry and distant from you and I know I can't change that. I can't feel loved and respected by someone who has to get his kicks watching other people have sex all the time. You didn't always do this. I'm asking you to go back to the way it was before—before you had online access to pornography.

ALEX: Fine, fine.

ALICIA: What does that mean?

ALEX: It means I'll stop, if that's what you want.

(Part of the problem is that he has no clue how his behavior has really impacted her. He's playing the victim role.)

ALICIA: You think I'm being unfair.

ALEX: You got that right.

ALEX: I'm wondering if you can put yourself in my shoes and consider how I must have been feeling all this time, knowing you prefer to look at other women for hours a week while we've grown more distant.

ALEX: I don't care about those women. And I don't think we're distant.

(This is not a debate. Her points are valid even if he disagrees.)

ALICIA: You spend more time with them than with me. But I'm not here to debate. I'm not saying I'm 100 percent right. I'm saying I'm not as close to you as a spouse should be and I resent it that you watch porn. And I'm worried we are growing further apart because I know I would stay distant from any person who preferred more time with sexy strangers than me. It simply has to change. Do you see any merit at all to what I'm saying?

(That last line is a good one. It forces him to look at what she's saying that he might agree with rather than focus on parts he disagrees with.)

ALEX: Yeah. I don't spend enough time with you. And I suppose if you were more interested in people online than with me I'd get jealous and upset, too.

(Good. Once they agree on something, they are that much closer to coming up with a plan to address it.)

ALICIA: Thank you. I propose that we ban online porn altogether. If that's too severe, I think you should examine why you feel a need to have it be a part of your life. And I propose we focus on ways in general to make our marriage stronger—more time together, going out more, that sort of thing. . . .

This discussion is probably the first of many. Alicia and Alex will need to have follow-up talks about the level of progress and determine what is working and what isn't. If he is addicted, he will revert to his ways and try to be cleverer in hiding it from her.

Chapter Eleven

Drinking

ACCORDING TO THE Center for the Advancement of Health, in any given year, a little more than 5 percent of the population will abuse alcohol regularly or be addicted to alcohol. Over the course of a lifetime, about 14 percent of adult Americans will become dependent on alcohol and over half will abuse alcohol at some point. About 40 percent of men and 20 percent of women reported alcohol-related problems in the past three years.

This chapter will focus exclusively on alcohol misuse and abuse but much of this information applies to other addictions, as well. Drug abuse, gambling, spending addictions, and sex addictions can be damaging to any family. The manner in which spouses address those problems often make matters worse—despite good intentions. This chapter, like all of the others, is designed to help you approach the problem—conversationally—in a useful way so that the difficulties can eventually be resolved or at least managed.

When Is Drinking a Problem?

Many young couples begin their relationship by going to bars or drinking socially. If the wife becomes pregnant she stops drinking—and her husband may or may not slow down his consumption of alcohol. According to an article in the May 2007 journal *Addiction*, couples who report drinking problems early on in their relationship have a higher divorce rate than couples who don't.

If you tell your spouse you're uncomfortable with the amount of alcohol she consumes and she not only takes you seriously but cuts back for good, you have a mature spouse and a solid relationship—and you must have approached the conversation in a good way. (Also, alcohol was likely not a real problem to begin with.) When drinking is a concern for at least one spouse, conversations are rarely that smooth. Most of the time the drinker gets defensive and the frequency and amount of alcohol consumption become a recurrent argument or debate.

When there is, in fact, a problem with alcohol, the drinker is likely to deny or minimize the problem and accuse the spouse of nagging or being too controlling. Abusers of alcohol rarely conclude that their drinking has gotten out of hand and excuse the occasional drunken night as either an exception to the rule ("It was a party . . . I usually never drink that much") or as an understandable action ("I had a stressful day. . . . My back is killing me"). Many abusers deny they are addicted so they minimize any periodic abuse of alcohol.

Signs of a Problem
If someone is dependent on alcohol, these are the indicators (only three—not all—are required for a diagnosis):

Withdrawal: When alcohol use is stopped, the addict suffers physical and psychological symptoms and requires more alcohol to alleviate those symptoms.

Tolerance: The user requires more and more alcohol to get the desired effect; the user can drink more without the more obvious signs of intoxication.

Unsuccessful Attempts to Quit: Despite promises and good intentions, someone dependent on alcohol will resume drinking after having "quit."

Cannot Limit Drinking: Usually, a desire to "just have one or two" results in the consumption of a lot more alcohol.

Alcohol Use Continues Despite Problems: Users may get in trouble on their jobs, with their spouses, or with the law, or develop medical problems and still persist in drinking.

Obligations Are Overlooked: Involvement with friends and family or obligations such as bill paying, child-rearing, and house chores are given a back seat to drinking.

"Blackouts" Are Experienced: Here the user awakens the next day with no memory of certain things that happened while drinking.

Someone who is abusing alcohol (but not addicted) and who is in denial about it will debate their spouse. They may even quote literature or point to sentences in this chapter (while overlooking others) to prove to you that drinking is not an issue—or at least not a serious issue. However, there is one question that if answered honestly is a reliable indicator that alcohol use has gotten out of hand: *Has any problem in your life recurred (such as marital disputes, diminished intimacy, driving infractions, less emotional or physical availability to one's children, money or legal problems, medical issues, embarrassing oneself in public, and so forth) because of your drinking?*

If the answer is yes, then an alcohol abuse problem exists—and the drinker is a step closer to dependency.

What You Need to Know to Help

If you are the spouse and you are worried (or at wits' end) about your partner's drinking, no doubt you have had many conversations about it—to no avail. There are two things you need to know:

- The longer the drinking has continued (and has been a source of concern), the more it is a real problem.
- The longer the drinking has been a problem, the more your marriage has organized around it, and the more likely your actions—unintentionally—have helped keep the problem going.

I'm not saying that the alcohol problem is caused by you. Nor am I saying that if you change the way you handle things, the problem drinker will improve. What I am saying is that you may have unwittingly helped to keep the marital car stuck in the mud, so to speak. If you change, things may or may not improve. If you don't change, matters are likely to stay the same or get worse (unless or until the problem drinker makes a significant positive change).

What do you need to change? First, examine how you may have dealt with the alcohol issue so far. You may be surprised to realize that some of your actions have enabled the drinker to continue drinking. Consider the following:

1. **You denied it.** Denial is common among alcohol abusers and also their spouses. The problem will never be addressed or changed if it is denied. Denial is one reason that most alcohol problems go on for years before they are addressed squarely.

2. **You tried to attack or control it.** This is common among spouses. It amounts to any of the following: arguing, cajoling, debating, threatening, pleading, punishing, insulting, crying, manipulating, and any other activity designed to force a spouse to see the error of his or her ways. It is a commonsense approach and doesn't work with alcohol abusers or addicts—otherwise you would have succeeded by now. This approach can become addictive in itself. Many spouses of alcohol abusers spend a great deal of emotional energy trying to "get" a partner to stop drinking (hiding alcohol, withdrawing love), typically to no avail.

3. **You pretended the problem wasn't so bad.** You knew there was a problem but you froze up, unsure of what to do, and ultimately you minimized the problem and decided to handle it sometime in the future if necessary.

4. **You gave up on yourself.** You became depressed. You felt hopeless and helpless and stuck. You saw no option but to put up with the situation.

There is a fifth way. It is not guaranteed to stop the alcohol abuse and improve the marriage. It is guaranteed to help you get unstuck so you have more control over your life (not control over your spouse's life—that effort must stop). However, it can result in you feeling better and *might* be the catalyst for the alcohol abuser to stop drinking. It might also result in the marriage collapsing if the drinker does nothing to change the alcohol problem. That's a sad but true reality.

Get the Help You Need

When alcohol has become a recurrent problem in a marriage, whether or not the user is addicted, the spouse of the user feels on the outside looking in. He feels a bit abandoned emotionally, is confused and unsure if his complaints about her drinking are valid, is tired of the entire issue, and has lost a sense of himself. Too much time is spent worrying about her drinking—or dealing with the aftereffects. Often there are real "what ifs." What if the marriage deteriorates? What will happen to the kids if the drinking continues? What if they get a divorce or separation? How can they afford that? It is precisely because of those legitimate concerns and others that spouses resort to pressure tactics designed to force the user to stop drinking.

The answer is to stop trying to control the spouse and start controlling yourself. You have to recognize when the alcohol abuser is using clever words to get you trapped in a no-win debate and be able to pull away from useless conversations. Mostly you have to learn the art of *detachment*.

Detachment is the ability to not become emotionally reactive when your buttons are getting pushed. It is an ability to care *about* without reflexively caring *for* (meaning a willingness to care that your spouse has a problem, to feel compassion, but not cover up for her or try to fix her or protect her from the negative consequences of her actions). It is a willingness to let the chips fall where they may where your spouse's drinking is concerned, otherwise you'll be enabling her. If she is too drunk to go to work, don't call the boss to say she has the flu. If she wrecks the car, don't tell neighbors you

Conversation Peace

What is an "intervention"? An intervention happens when a group of loved ones—friends and family—lovingly confront an abuser of alcohol by stating how the alcohol use has harmed or hurt them. It is harder for an addict to manipulate an entire group. The group uses their collective power to gain leverage—hopefully—so that the alcohol user will get help. Members involved in the intervention make it clear that they will no longer support alcohol abuse, but they will be helpful and supportive of the recovery process. For more detailed information on how to conduct an intervention, read *Love First* by Jeff and Debra Jay.

did it. If she leaves a mess, let her clean it up. If she buys liquor, don't try to hide it or dispose of it. It goes without saying that if the drinker's behaviors put you or your children at risk for physical harm, you must take action to prevent that. Staying aloof while your kids are in the car with a drunk driver is not what I mean by detachment. Any time a severe injury is possible you must take action. Would you be willing to contact the police if you knew for sure that your spouse was driving drunk?

Seven Guaranteed Outcomes

Much is unpredictable when dealing with an alcoholic, but there are certain outcomes that are guaranteed.

1. If you do nothing and pretend, the drinker will drink.

2. If you act with hostility, the drinker will use your anger as an excuse to drink—and blame you for it.

3. If you dispose of liquor, the drinker will find better hiding places.

4. If you try to be tolerant and loving to show what a devoted and unconditionally accepting spouse you are, the drinker will drink—then feel guilty because you've been so nice—and drink some more to cope with the guilt.

5. If you pull away out of disgust, the drinker—being highly sensitive to rejection—will drink.

6. If you try to detach as a maneuver to get the drinker to stop drinking the drinker will drink and you will stop detaching because you will conclude detachment does not work. Detachment is not done to stop a drinker from drinking; it is done for your sake only—to stop you from allowing your spouse's use of alcohol to be the center of your life.

7. If you detach to help yourself, then the drinker will suffer more pain and may eventually get help or stop drinking. If she doesn't stop, you will be stronger and more able to effectively contend with whatever life changes you decide must be made.

Good Openings

If your spouse misuses alcohol on occasion (but is not dependent upon alcohol and has had no serious consequences—yet—to her drinking) and readily admits that she has a tendency to drink too much here or there, it's possible that straightforward discussions about your concerns can help. The proof is in the pudding. If these opening comments ultimately result in no changes—or in the situation worsening—then the problem is not minor and recurrent efforts to get her to see the light may fail.

If speaking to a spouse who only occasionally misuses alcohol, state clearly what you observe and what your concerns are. Ask for some ideas on what can be done.

- "Honey, I don't think you have a drinking problem but I am getting increasingly concerned when you do drink. You drink more than you used to and I get the impression you've started looking forward to your wine at night. Can we discuss this further?"
- "I've noticed you've gone from having a glass of wine a night with dinner to two or three glasses. That concerns me. I'd like to discuss it and see why it is you want to drink more."
- "It seems that whenever we go out socially lately you drink more than you ever have and I have to be the designated driver. Your drinking really worries me. I don't like it. I'd like to discuss what to do about it."
- "Every time you drink in the evening to relax I feel disconnected from you. You're not as involved with the kids at night and you seem to be more in your own world. I'm not happy with the situation. Can we discuss this now?"

Good Follow-Throughs

Your spouse may get a little defensive. However, if the marriage is sound and your spouse agrees that she has been drinking more than usual, she will agree to a plan to limit alcohol intake. If that plan fails, or if your spouse is far more defensive, more talking is necessary. Stick to facts and to how the drinking affects you. Don't make accusations that your spouse can easily debate.

- "You said you'd cut back on your drinking. You did at first but that lasted only about a week. Now I'm really concerned. Either you have a problem controlling your drinking or you are bothered by something else. We need to talk about this."
- "I'm not overlooking the fact that you resumed drinking again. I know you think I'm making a big deal out of this and I'm no expert. All I know is that I pull away from you emotionally when you drink as often as you do. Please, let's figure out a way for you to drink less."
- "I hear you when you say that you don't have a problem with alcohol and that getting a buzz on a weekend night is perfectly acceptable. But when you have a buzz on I'm left being in charge of everything while you withdraw. I don't like that and I don't think it's fair. Something has to change."
- "I'm not telling you what to do. I'm asking you to respect my concerns and meet me halfway. I don't like what's happening. What are you willing to do?"

When Drinking Is a Serious Problem: More Good Openings

Here you are at a new level. You are now aware that your spouse's drinking is highly problematic (alcohol abuse or dependency) and you have had conversations that have gotten you nowhere. Your tendency will be to say what you've already said many times before—only more intensely, or with greater drama, or with bigger threats.

That approach will always fail.

Now your words must be designed to help you practice detachment. And remember, don't try to detach as a clever tactic to get your spouse to stop drinking—that's not detachment, that's you fooling yourself—and you won't fool your alcohol-abusing spouse. You must detach as a way to get you unhooked from the tug-of-war you are in with your spouse. Your tone must be straightforward and calm, not punitive or insulting.

- "I've made a decision. I'm not going to talk to you about your drinking anymore, and I'm not going to involve myself in anything even remotely connected to your drinking. I love you and wish things could be different, but I have to look out for myself from now on."
- "No, I'm not going to call your boss and tell her you have the flu."
- "I'll be home in a few hours. I have an Al-Anon meeting tonight."
- "I thought I'd share with you this list of new things I'd like to do, organizations I'd like to join, hobbies I'd be interested in. I want to be more involved in things that will make me feel good."
- "You're right. I didn't clean up the mess you made last night. It's not my job."
- "Last night I didn't stay awake wondering where you were. It really feels good not to worry."

When Drinking Is a Serious Problem: More Good Follow-Throughs

The follow-through is key when conversing with alcohol abusers. They will do all they can to render you impotent. They will blame you, ignore you, turn your accusations around on you, bring up irrelevant issues—in short, do anything to keep you from getting the upper hand. Here you'll find a list of excuses the drinker might make, as well as possible replies for you.

- If the drinker says, "You don't trust me" you reply, "I don't trust your judgment when it concerns alcohol."
- If the drinker says, "At least I keep my job" (and that is what is called a permission-giving belief; it is merely an excuse to justify drinking) you reply, "That doesn't change the fact that you abuse alcohol and our life together has fallen apart. You can do what you choose; I have to consider my choices, as well."
- If the drinker says, "I only drink on weekends," you reply, "All I know is that our life together isn't working as long as you drink the way you do." (This is a good response because you aren't getting caught up in the specifics of the argument. You are repeating that alcohol consumption has gotten out of hand.)
- If the drinker says, "It could be worse. I could be doing cocaine and wiping out our savings," you reply, "Your drinking is still a problem for me. I have to decide what I'm willing to tolerate."
- If the drinker says, "I drink because you stress me out," you say, "The point is you drink—to excess. And I can't ignore that anymore."

Sample Script

Pete has been drinking to excess for seven years. He works with computers for a *Fortune* 500 company. To friends and outsiders he is friendly. At home he is often irritable, sometimes a tyrant. Recently, Jane started attending Al-Anon, a support group for family members of alcoholics. She is learning how to detach and not get caught up in Pete's drinking habits. She is scared, too. She wonders if her marriage can last. You can't tell from just the printed words, but Jane's tone is nonthreatening in this conversation. She is matter-of-fact; no hint of sarcasm or disgust in her voice.

JANE: I've started attending Al-Anon. I have another meeting tonight.

PETE: You've already attended some meetings and you're just telling me about it now? No wonder we have problems.

JANE: I should be home after nine.

(Appropriately, she ignored his comment and didn't take the bait.)

PETE: A bunch of people sitting together blaming their spouses. That's all that is.

JANE: Actually, I feel really understood and supported.

PETE: Right. Aren't you taking this whole thing a bit too far?

JANE: I don't understand.

PETE: I've told you for years that my drinking—while maybe it goes against your sensibilities—hasn't really caused problems. But now you're taking it to the next level where everyone will agree with you and make me out to be the bad guy.

JANE: I'm not calling you the bad guy. I used to think that.

PETE: You changed your mind?

JANE: I hated it when all I could focus on was your drinking. You were the bad guy before. Now I'm thinking about what makes me happy and what I need to do to be less depressed. Actually, my goal is to try not to think of you so much.

PETE: There you go with the threats. You've been telling me for years—ordering me practically—not to drink. Now you make threats. Al-Anon is doing wonders for you.

(He is very adept at turning the issue back on her.)

JANE: Funny, but I don't see myself as threatening you. I'm not thinking what I should or shouldn't do about you. I'm thinking about what I need to do for me.

PETE: Oh, so you've learned how to be selfish.

JANE: And for the first time in a long time I feel better. I've ignored myself for too long. I've looked online and there are some courses I intend to take. I intend to finish my degree.

PETE: Another secret? When were you planning on telling me that?

JANE: I'm just focused on myself. I'll let you take care of yourself; I'll stay out of your way so that I have more time and energy to think about what I want to do.

PETE: That doesn't sound like a marriage. It sounds like ships passing in the night.

JANE: I guess it does. But I'll still be with you, for now anyway. I still enjoy watching movies with you. But I'm giving up trying to get you to stop drinking. That's what you wanted, right? And I have more time for me.

PETE: I'm not going to AA. You can forget that.

JANE: I didn't say a word about AA. Go or don't go. It's your choice.

PETE: I don't fit in there. Some of those guys have serious problems, I mean serious—like losing their jobs. Some even beat their wives. I'd never do that.

(That was a veiled threat. Ordinarily such a comment would make Jane passive.)

JANE: I've learned in Al-Anon that any physical threat is unacceptable and the police must be called.

PETE: What's that supposed to mean?

JANE: I won't debate you anymore. It exhausts me. Go to AA or don't go. It really doesn't matter to me like it used to.

PETE: Like I really believe that.

JANE: You don't have to believe it. What you believe isn't my concern right now. My goal is to make myself happier. I want to take some courses, maybe get a whole new career. I'm taking up tennis lessons—I guess I forgot to mention that.

PETE: *(Studying her closely)* I know what you're doing. You can't fool me.

JANE: And I know what *you're* doing by saying that. And you know what? I don't really care. It's water down my back. It's okay if you try to throw me off balance or sidestep the problem of your drinking. I'm just thinking about my future now and what I need. The beer is in the fridge. Help yourself to as many as you want. Or don't. I'm going out to my meeting. See you later.

Coping with a problem drinker or with someone who has an addiction requires patience and a determination to set limits for what you will and won't tolerate. It is not easy. But the right kind of conversation can keep you from getting off balance.

Chapter Twelve

Unfulfilled Dreams

MOST COUPLES HAVE a set of expectations—sometimes unspoken—about how their lives will proceed over the next many years. Maybe they'll buy a new house, or retire and relocate to some sunny climate. Maybe they look forward to having children or to climbing the career ladder or going back to school. But then one spouse has a change of heart.

- "I want to start having children sooner than we planned. I can't wait another three years."
- "I want to change careers and go back to school, even if it means we'll have money problems for a while."
- "I'm not happy where we live. I want to move."
- "My father can't live by himself. We should invite him to stay with us."
- "I'd like to retire early. I know that will affect our finances but I don't think I can last another five years."
- "I was offered a job promotion. It's everything I've ever wanted, but it means moving to the other side of the country away from our friends and family."

- "I'm tired of wasting money on in-vitro fertilization procedures that haven't worked. I say we give up trying to have children."
- "I want to quit my job and stay home with the kids. We'll just have to downsize."

So much for long-range planning. Now what?

Can You Cope with Unexpected Changes?

When a spouse does a one-eighty over agreed-upon future plans, partners are not just disappointed—they usually feels like the rug was pulled out from underneath them. One middle-aged childless couple had saved money to fund an overseas adoption. It had been the woman's dream. As the process started to bog down and take longer than expected her husband changed his mind. He stated that his dream had always been to buy a vacation home. If the adoption went through, he'd have to wait "perhaps forever" to buy the home he always wanted. The woman was crushed. "It's like a betrayal" she said to me. "I could force the issue, I suppose. But do I really want my husband to go along with something he truly doesn't want? What if he resents me forever?"

And it's no picnic for the one who changes his mind, either. One man promised to move out west so that his wife could be closer to her family. Then he had to tell her he couldn't go through with it. "I agonized for days before I told my wife there was no way I could give up my job and move. I worked too hard to get where I am with the company. She told me I cared more about status and career than I did about her. That's not fair. But . . . could she be right?"

Unexpected changes in plans happen, but if they are managed properly you can avoid sending your marriage into a tailspin.

When Plans Get Turned Upside-Down

When there is an abrupt turn of events over future plans and spouses have strong and different preferences as to what should happen, compromises aren't always practical. You can choose this path or that path but there may be no middle ground. When couples finally agree on a course of action, they are betting that the "loser" won't harbor resentment, which can slowly poison the relationship. Therefore it requires a great deal of maturity on the part of the couple to live with their decision and try to make the best of it.

When your dreams for the future are dashed—or put on hold indefinitely—do you think you'll be able to handle it? What personal strengths or weaknesses will come to bear on the situation? If you can't make up your mind, ask yourself the following true or false questions. If you feel that even 51 percent of the time the statement is true, answer true. And be honest because this quiz will only help you in the long run.

"We need

Answer True or False.

1. *I was a responsible child growing up.*
2. *Because of certain family problems, I had to learn to grow up quickly.*
3. *I often worried about other family members when I was a child.*
4. *I'm too concerned with what other people think.*
5. *I tend to back down during arguments.*
6. *I resent being told what to do.*
7. *I tend to be right about things.*

8. *If I feel strongly about something important, I want my spouse to go along with my views.*
9. *I resent it when I don't get my way.*
10. *When it comes down to it, there's a right way and a wrong way to do things.*
11. *During an argument, one of us shuts down and the other keeps wanting to talk.*
12. *When we disagree, my spouse and I debate who's wrong or right.*
13. *I feel taken for granted a lot by my spouse.*
14. *If I have a complaint, my spouse tends to think I'm making mountains out of molehills.*
15. *I don't often look forward to seeing my spouse at the end of the day.*

to talk"

These statements measure three areas that will help you to determine how well you can handle unexpected, unwanted changes: past experiences, personality, and communication skills.

The first five statements deal with your past. The more you answered "True" to those five questions, you may indeed have the capacity to put aside your needs for the sake of others. The problem is that you may have given so much of yourself to others in the past (while putting your needs aside) that you yearn to have someone else make sacrifices for you now. As a result, you may resent your partner (or feel depressed) if you have to give up something that is important to you and may inwardly wonder "When will it be my turn?" If your needs were regularly met growing up you may find it easier to make sacrifices for your spouse now.

Statements six through ten measure how rigid or flexible you can be. If you answered "True" to most of those you have a need to be right, don't see much gray area, and can feel entitled to get your way. Consequently, you will have a harder time making a major sacrifice for your spouse if you don't see the logic of it. You may be more concerned with practical aspects of a decision more than the emotional aspects.

The final five statements tap into the communication skills you and your spouse possess as well as the overall level of goodwill you two have. If you feel taken for granted and don't often look forward to seeing one another at day's end, goodwill is low and it will be difficult to make a major sacrifice for your spouse's sake. In addition, if your communication skills need improving, you will struggle trying to have a constructive dialogue about a major divisive issue.

Good Openings

The immediate goal is to state clearly what it is you'd like to happen while showing sympathy for the fact that your spouse may be in for a major letdown.

- "I know we've spoken about trying to have children this year but now I'm not sure that's what I want. I'd like to talk about why I've reconsidered. I'm sorry. I know this must upset you."
- "I've been thinking a lot about my mother, you know I worry about her. As disruptive as it might be, I'd like us to consider having her live with us. I'm sure it's not something you really want, but let's discuss it further and weigh all of our options."

- "Before either of us makes a decision, could we discuss the pros and cons?"
- "This won't be the last time we talk about this. But if we put our feelings on the table now we can sort through them and hopefully make a decision we can both live with."
- "Please don't give in so easily to my request. I'm grateful, but I want us to be sure we can live with the final decision without resentments. Take more time to think about how you really feel."
- "I don't blame you for feeling angry. I know it seems like I'm going back on our agreement but after thinking more about it I have a lot of concerns."

Good Follow-Throughs

When a couple may have to do an about-face over a major life course, tensions can mount. Follow-through talks need to focus on getting clarity about the benefits and costs (emotionally and otherwise) of whatever decision must get made as well as deal sensitively with emotions during the conversation. When exasperated or scared, avoid making idle threats. If you find you are getting nowhere in your conversations—merely bashing your heads against a wall—you need to try a different approach.

One key rule to keep in mind: People are reluctant to make difficult changes that others want them to make unless they first feel understood and secondly feel cared about. Threats, name-calling, shouting matches, punitive measures, or any effort designed to force a spouse to go along with your wishes rarely makes the spouse feel understood—let alone cared about. At best, your spouse will go along with your wishes and deeply resent you. At worst there will be a standoff, goodwill will deteriorate, and the marriage may be at risk.

"We need to talk"

Conversation Peace

One of the better ways to reduce arguments and enhance closeness is to make sure you have at least fifteen minutes a day for pleasant, focused chitchat about noncontroversial topics (not while you're distracted by the kids, TV, the computer, and so on). Your aim is to chat about these and other ordinary topics and show interest and mutual support. Ideally, you might engage in these conversations while cuddling together, offering a back rub, taking a stroll—something that makes you feel connected. When done successfully, these small dialogues serve as an inoculation against future arguments. Friendly chitchat where each person feels listened to and cared about makes it more likely that a future disagreement will be less intense than it otherwise would be.

- "Just for the sake of discussion, if things were to go my way, what would need to happen for you so that you wouldn't be depressed or resentful? And in the same way, I want to think about what could happen for me if I didn't get my way."
- "If you're angry that I changed my mind and things may not go as you had planned, I understand. If you're angry because of how I feel, that's not something I can easily help. How I feel is how I feel."
- "Just because each of us feels strongly about we want, doesn't mean we can't give way to what the other one wants."
- "Are we overlooking any compromises that would work for both of us?"

- "All we do is debate and try to make each other wrong. Neither one of us is wrong for feeling the way we do. Somehow we have to find merit in each other's point of view so that we don't feel like adversaries."

- "Let's discuss this by switching roles. I'll defend your position and you defend mine."

- "You keep telling me I must not care about you unless I go along with what you want. That isn't fair. I could say the same thing about you but it would not be true and would get us nowhere. The bottom line is we love each other but we both can't get what we want with this decision. One of us has to give up a dream."

- "It seems like after we discuss this we end up in a bad mood and avoid each other. I suggest that we do the opposite. Even if our conversations get us angry, we each need to make a sincere effort to stay connected afterwards—to show affection and try to be nice."

- "You keep accusing me of going back on my word. I don't look at it that way. Yes, I have changed my mind but I'm not insisting we do things my way. I'm saying I've reconsidered things and we need to reopen the discussion. I still might go along with our original plan."

Sample Script

Mike and Patty have been married five years. They had planned to start having children by now but Mike wants to delay it for another few years. He is thinking of leaving his job in computer programming and earning a master's degree in education so he can teach high school. He's afraid that if Patty gets pregnant he'll be forced to stay with his programming job—something he's grown to dislike—and may never get his teaching degree. Patty thinks that having children should be their priority since she is now thirty-two years old. They've had this discussion several times, resulting only in ill will.

As with all scripts in this book, the point here is not to provide a solution—there is no answer that applies to every couple. It is the process of the conversation—not the outcome—that is most important.

MIKE: We've been over this. You know how I feel. Why do you keep bringing it up?

PATTY: Because it isn't resolved.

MIKE: The only way it will be resolved for you is if you get your way.

PATTY: And that's true for you, as well. But the bigger concern is what happens to us after only one of us gets our way?

(Patty is correctly looking at the bigger picture. It's not just about whether to have children or not. It's about maintaining a committed, loving relationship despite the fact that one of them will have to make a sacrifice he or she would rather not make.)

MIKE: Are you saying that if I don't agree to start having kids right now we might not make it?

PATTY: I'm not threatening you, if that's what you mean. I'm just worried. The way we've gone about this is to debate one another; try to win the other one over with persuasion. It hasn't worked and it's only made us more annoyed.

MIKE: Because we only talk about what we don't agree on. When it comes to starting a family, what *do* we agree on? Not on the timing, that's for sure.

(Mike is starting to see the bigger picture. When couples disagree, it can be helpful to focus first on what they do agree on. That way they can start to feel like teammates instead of adversaries.)

PATTY: We both agree we want to have children someday.

MIKE: Right.

PATTY: And I think we both want our love to be strong no matter what we decide now. After all, if one of us has to make a sacrifice it helps to feel that it's worth it.

MIKE: It'd be lousy if we make a decision and the one who doesn't win has a bad attitude.

PATTY: I agree. But I feel uneasy about the word *win*. That implies that one of us loses.

MIKE: Well, if you're saying it needs to be a win-win situation, that really can't happen. The best that can happen is that no one holds any grudges.

PATTY: Okay. But maybe we can compromise. For example, I'm willing to wait one more year—but just one—before we try to get pregnant. That gives you time to work on your master's degree. Besides, there's no guarantee I'd get pregnant right away. You might have even more time.

MIKE: That doesn't work for me.

(Mike failed to appreciate that Patty was trying to be flexible. Fortunately, he corrects himself.)

MIKE: Let me try that again. You're trying to find a compromise and I really appreciate that. And maybe it's a good idea. I have to think about it more. But my initial reaction is that I prefer to be settled into a teaching job before we have kids. Otherwise, I'll always be worrying about income and feel pressure to work more hours and take a longer time to get my degree.

PATTY: I think that's the crux of it. Your main value is having all the financial ducks in a row. I know it's because you want us to be a happy family that's well provided for. But my main value isn't finances. The money will work out. My value is starting a family while we're young enough to have two or three kids. We don't need job security to be happy. Most people don't have job security.

(Patty and Mike have split their concerns. Patty is focused on the emotional well-being of the family—having a loving family regardless of circumstances—while Mike is focusing on the practical side of things.)

MIKE: Is there any way out of this?

PATTY: We could find a compromise. Otherwise I suggest we take time away from the issue—perhaps a week or two—and really consider each other's views rather than only focusing on our own views.

(Mike and Patty succeeded in making their conversation less volatile and more respectful. Each pointed out some merit to the other's ideas which helped reduce defensiveness and allowed each to feel a bit more understood. That makes it more likely that goodwill will be present no matter what the final decision.)

Chapter Thirteen

Cheating

STATISTICS ON INFIDELITY vary. The Kinsey studies and Hite report suggest that in up to 70 percent of all marriages a spouse will cheat. A major study by the University of Chicago in the 1990s was more optimistic, suggesting that infidelity occurs in no more than 25 percent of all marriages. When you add to the fact that the definition of infidelity varies (some studies require a sexual relationship, others include "emotional infidelity") then the real numbers are fuzzy. However, experts tend to agree that cheating will occur in 30 to 40 percent of all marriages. On the brighter side, some affairs occur after a marriage has all but died and weren't the cause of the marital problems.

It tends to be true (not always, of course) that men start affairs for sex—and it may or may not become emotional. Women are more likely to have affairs for emotional reasons. There are many types of affairs, and all can be devastating. Some people have cybersex with an online stranger. Some chat online with a "friend" and start developing feelings although there is no sex. Some people have purely sexual affairs. Some have emotional affairs that have not become sexual but there are sexual fantasies, secret get-togethers, phone conversations, a passion to spend time with that person—all of which are usually hidden from a spouse. And finally some people have affairs that are both sexual and emotional.

Regardless of the type of affair, any affair can seriously damage a marriage. That is because all affairs involve deceit and secrecy—both of which significantly undermine trust.

Cheating 101

Every spouse who is a victim of an affair wants to know "Why did it happen?" I have yet to hear an unfaithful spouse provide an answer that makes a partner respond, "That makes sense." In other words, no answer is usually acceptable. In fact, any answer makes the unfaithful spouse sound like he or she is justifying the affair—which only makes the partner madder.

Still, an affair happens most often for the following reasons:

Sex addiction or character flaws. A philanderer may feel entitled to cheat. Someone addicted to sex may feel compelled to cheat while wishing to stop. In all cases, the wandering spouse made a conscious choice to cheat.

Unintentional involvements. Many people develop friendships that truly start out innocent. Over time the friends look forward to time together, begin discussing personal problems or future dreams, and start to develop feelings. Many deny that an affair has started because no sex is involved. On closer examination, it becomes clear that each person made small, step-by-step decisions to spend more time together and to be secretive about the nature or frequency of those meetings or conversations. Or, a person may have an unexpected "one-night stand" especially if alcohol was consumed and a spouse is unaware of what might be going on.

A less-than-satisfying marriage. In fact, an "OK" marriage is vulnerable to an affair almost as much as an unhappy marriage. An unhappy spouse may get involved with another to feel listened to, cared about, have more passionate sex, or be better treated. Or the person may be wondering if in fact "the grass is greener" and is exploring "what's out there."

Tit-for-tat. Some people cheat to get back at an unfaithful spouse or to punish a spouse for some other disliked behavior (the spouse is too jealous, too controlling, is abusive, drinks too much, and so forth).

Overwhelmed by life circumstances. Some people cheat when a baby is on the way, or a parent dies, or when the kids leave home. In such cases, these life transitions hit a nerve for that individual and trigger a need to perhaps "feel young again" or to cope better with overwhelming feelings.

There are numerous possible other reasons. For example, people who marry at a young age are more likely to have an affair than people who are older when they get married. Someone afraid of deep intimacy might cheat on his wife as a way to regulate his level of emotional closeness.

The Immediate Consequences of an Affair

When an affair is discovered, the damage is not just in one area of the marriage. A partner doesn't think "We still have a great marriage and you are a good person except in this one area of infidelity." Affairs shatter the entire foundation of a marriage. Everything that was good is at risk for crumbling. Affairs splinter the image a spouse has of the now-unfaithful partner. "I thought I knew the kind of person you were," a distraught spouse claims, "but I don't know you at all!" It can be frightening for the betrayed spouse to realize that the partner once viewed as honest, upstanding, moral, and devoted to family life seems to be totally different.

After the affair, it's extremely hard for the victim to want to connect warmly. Usually there is hostility and perhaps loathing. At best there is silent contempt. The victim often obsesses about the affair, doesn't trust that the entire story has been told, expects more lies, and interrogates the spouse repeatedly. Positive memories of family vacations, holidays, Valentine's Day gifts, all become suspect. "When we were vacationing at the beach last summer, did you spend your time wishing you could be with *her?*" Petty annoyances that happen in any marriage—the spouse arrives home late, forgets a grocery item, doesn't have time to tidy up the house—all become reasons to lash out. For many couples, making love is now impossible. For others, making love becomes highly passionate—followed the next day by the betrayed spouse acting cold. All of that happens even when the unfaithful spouse is truly repentant and wanting to heal the marriage. Just as often, though, the unfaithful spouse still has feelings for the other person and may have doubts about the desire to stay married. That only adds to the couple's misery as they slog through their days trying to hold the marriage together.

Phases of Repair

Couples who are motivated to heal the marriage after an affair can succeed. If you are one of those couples who choose to stay in the marriage you can expect to have dozens of conversations about the affair and how to rebuild the marriage. It can be exhausting but is a necessary part of healing.

There are three broad phases a couple experiences after an affair and conversations will be different depending upon the phase. These phases tend to overlap and a person can be in two phases or even all three phases at one time. Usually, one phase tends to predominate.

1. **The Roller-Coaster Phase.** Here emotions are wild, conversations are heated, and optimism is almost absent. This phase is filled with conversations about what really happened and why. Blaming and attacking is common. Many of the rules of good conversation I wrote about in past chapters get tossed aside. The victim usually finds it impossible to speak calmly and respectfully. Name-calling, put-downs, and other forms of verbal attacks are typical. The unfaithful spouse is best advised to be understanding and accepting of such verbal lashings as much as possible. Calling them unfair or hurtful won't work. The victim will only respond, "But what you did to me was unfair and hurtful!"

2. **The Depressed-Accepting Phase.** Here the betrayed spouse has finally accepted the affair and has begun to learn to live with it—however painfully. That spouse is grieving the loss of faithfulness in the marriage, is probably coping with a damaged self-image, and is trying to slowly rebuild trust. Occasional mood swings may happen but for the most part things have started to settle down—although a bit grimly. Here the couple has a sluggish coexistence punctuated by occasional nice days or moments together.

3. **The Rebirth Phase.** Here trust is on the rise and the marriage is looked upon more favorably than unfavorably. The affair is regarded as a painful time but the unfaithful partner is viewed in

a more positive light overall. The affair may not be forgotten but every day the betrayed spouse makes a choice to be forgiving.

Good Openings and Follow-Throughs: The Roller-Coaster Phase

This phase usually lasts anywhere from three to six months, but sometimes lasts longer. It goes on longer than it should when the unfaithful spouse quickly grows weary of the interrogations and the tense home life and develops a "get over it" attitude. Then his spouse thinks "He has no clue what I'm going through," and progress stalls. Unless the unfaithful spouse is being physically abused or emotionally battered, he or she is best advised to "take your lumps" and nurture the attitude that the betrayed spouse has every right to feel the way he or she does. However, the betrayed spouse is best advised to use caution when verbally attacking or berating the unfaithful spouse.

Vicious attacks, however justified, can turn a remorseful, shameful spouse into an angry, blaming, defiant spouse who may question whether he wants to remain in a marriage where he is so unrelentingly attacked.

Talk Alert

Once an affair is revealed the unfaithful spouse says he will tell the truth but then sometimes withholds information about the affair that would be embarrassing, painful to the spouse, or get him in more trouble (such as the fact that his former mistress called him at work the day before). Openness is essential. Maintaining secrecy almost always backfires.

If You Are the Victim of an Affair, Say the Following

- "I know I've asked you these questions before and I'll probably ask them again until I feel more trusting. Bear with me."
- "When I ask you all of the details of the kind of sex you and he had, you tell me 'That's disgusting' and refuse to answer. I'm sorry but I need to know the specifics." (Some betrayed spouses do need to know graphic details of sexual encounters while others would rather not know. It is a good idea to put that information on hold. If it is still important to know weeks later, it can be revisited.)
- "Yes, I've checked your cell phone bills and I found some e-mails you sent to your girlfriend. You accuse me of spying on you and going through your private things. I don't like doing it but until I feel more trusting I will continue to do so." (Secretly checking up on a spouse who was unfaithful can offer reassurances in the short term. If done for an extended period of time a spouse can become addicted to seeking evidence rather than relying on other aspects of the marriage to restore trust.)
- "If your boyfriend tries to contact you in any way I need you to tell me about it. I promise not to be mad at you, but I won't put up with you two having more secret conversations."
- "When I call you and ask you where you are, you get mad thinking I'm checking up on you. Sometimes I am because I don't trust you. But sometimes I'm not. I'm sure it's no fun for you that I do this but it isn't pleasant for me either."
- "It may seem to you that all I do is attack you. There are many times I don't say a word and many times when you're not here that I'm in pain thinking about what happened. For every hour we talk about it I've probably spent ten hours agonizing over it. I need you to understand that."

- "I feel a strong need to attack you and turn my back on you. And at the same time I hate feeling that way. Nothing I do feels right. I wish you'd understand that."
- "I know it looks like I'm giving you contradictory messages when one day I'm getting along with you and the next day I'm not. My feelings really are mixed. Please bear with me."
- "I want you to try to get closer to me and at the same time I want you to keep your distance. That means I need more time to sort through my feelings. Right now I hate you *and* I love you."

If You Are the Unfaithful Spouse, Say the Following

- "I'll answer any questions truthfully. But sometimes when I say 'I don't know' I'm speaking the truth. I didn't always analyze why I did things at the time I did them." (Sometimes the unfaithful spouse doesn't recall specific dates, times, and details, and "I don't know" is an honest answer.)
- "I can't blame you for mistrusting me and I understand why you need to ask so many questions."
- "You can check my cell phone and e-mails anytime. Whatever it takes for you to feel more trusting." (Never argue about the "invasion of my privacy.")
- "I'm always willing to discuss the affair. But I also want to discuss our marriage as a whole. I want to find ways to make it better overall."
- "Even though I didn't have a sexual affair, I shouldn't have let things get so far emotionally."
- "I apologize but at the same time feel that no apology could ever begin to heal the damage I've done."

Conversation Peace

After several weeks of the roller-coaster phase it can be a good idea to schedule talks about the affair rather than have them occur at random times. This allows the faithful spouse the opportunity to vent feelings and ask questions. This also keeps the unfaithful partner from having to worry about unscheduled surprise conversations, which can ruin an otherwise pleasant time together. The talks should not be more than an hour. The unfaithful spouse must agree to cooperate and not become frustrated or sarcastic at hearing some of the same questions again. When the time is up the couple should try to not let bad feelings linger.

Good Openings and Follow-Throughs: The Depressed-Accepting Phase

Here the emotional ups and downs have given way to flat feelings. Neither spouse is happy, both are exhausted emotionally, and each is wondering if the marriage can ever be good again. Each needs a little hope and a little laughter. It is here that some degree of forgiveness begins to take root.

If You Are the Victim of an Affair, Say the Following

- "I'm not as angry as I once was and that's progress. But I'm not as happy as I want to be. My energy for you right now is kind of low so you'll have to bear with me."

- "We had a nice day today. I'm glad of that. I still have bad days but I'm hoping we'll have more like today."
- "Every time you check your cell phone messages I get a twinge of fear and anger. I trust you more than I did, but I can't help feeling this way sometimes."
- "I feel a lot better today than I did six months ago. I guess that's progress."
- "I like it a lot when you go out of your way to ask me how I'm feeling about all of this. It lets me know you care and I don't feel like I'm always the one bringing the topic up."
- "Sometimes I don't want to feel better because as soon as I do you'll think you're off the hook. That's not a fair way to think. I guess I worry you'll take for granted all I've had to go through."

If You Are the Unfaithful Spouse, Say the Following

- "I know you won't forget what happened. But I won't either. I'll always keep somewhere in mind what happened and how it affected you." (The unfaithful spouse usually wants the entire affair to be forgotten and to remain in the past. However, the more the unfaithful spouse can remember what happened and its impact, the less the betrayed spouse has a reason to.)
- "I'm happy that you seem to be feeling somewhat better. But I'm not underestimating all you've been through."
- "Thanks for getting this far along with me."

Good Openings and Follow-Throughs: The Rebirth Phase

Here the couple makes a clear recommitment to each other. The future looks brighter. Some bad days may show up but they are less frequent. External reminders of what happened (from watching a movie or hearing about a celebrity affair) aren't so difficult anymore.

- "What I really appreciate about you is. . . ."
- "I'm happy we stayed together through all this."
- "When you see that I'm feeling down, you're no longer afraid to come up and give me a hug or ask me what's wrong. I like that."
- "I forgive you but some days I still get furious."
- "What I've gained through this experience is. . . ."
- "I think we're stronger as a couple in these ways. . . ."
- "My trust of you isn't 100 percent yet. Some days I'll have some insecure feelings. I hope you can understand."

Sample Script
"We need to talk"

The content of the script will vary depending upon which phase of healing the couple is in. In the roller-coaster phase, the betrayed spouse is intently focused on what happened, why it happened, whether it is still happening, and whether it could happen again. The betrayed spouse may also be wondering if the marriage is sustainable. At that phase, the unfaithful spouse is sincerely regretting what happened (or not—in which case the marriage will probably not last) and may still have feelings for the other person. As stated earlier, it is helpful if the couple schedules their conversations during this phase. Random, spontaneous discussions can be overwhelming because they occur with high intensity and frequency and there is never any predictable "down time."

The end of the roller-coaster phase and the beginning of the acceptance phase is where the marriage can turn in a decidedly positive or negative direction. Here the intense fighting has greatly subsided so conversations can be more productive.

Consider this situation: Frank cheated on Linda after eight years of marriage. Two months have passed since Linda found out about the affair. Conversations are less volatile now but goodwill is still too low. Each feels exhausted.

LINDA: I know we're trying to just get along without much tension. But some days all I think about is what you did. And I'm supposed to suck it up and try to get over it for the sake of our marriage. It feels very unfair.

FRANK: We've talked about this. . . .

LINDA: I know. I'm not supposed to turn a good day into a bad one by bringing up my feelings. Highly unfair.

FRANK: I just think we've talked about it every which way we can. We never get anywhere by talking.

(This is a mistake by Frank. What Linda wants to hear is understanding and compassion; what he's communicating is that it's wrong for her to feel what she feels.)

LINDA: Imagine a good friend of yours was grieving the death of someone he loved. And it was months later and you saw him visibly upset and he wanted to talk. Would you tell him he has to move on? Or would you listen with compassion?

FRANK: I'd listen.

LINDA: That's what I want from you. I need to know that my pain matters to you. I'm finished asking questions and wondering why you did such a thing. But my pain hasn't gone away. When you care about that it helps.

FRANK: I know. I'm sorry. I think what's happening is that when I see you in pain I get upset with myself; I feel guilty. But the way I handle it is to want you to not feel what you're feeling. That's not right.

LINDA: You want me to "move on." I want to move in a direction where I know I'm cared about, not where I'm made to feel bad for my feelings.

FRANK: I'll be more understanding.

(Frank was wise not to add something like "But you have to understand how I feel. . . . ")

LINDA: It's strange. I want to feel better, for us to be happier. But on days when I feel that way I also resent you even more. Somehow when I feel better I worry that you will think that what you did wasn't that serious—and I don't want you to minimize what you did.

FRANK: I won't. The last few months have been hell. I want you to feel better and us to have a great marriage. But that doesn't mean that what I did wasn't a big deal. It's just that I want you to know I do regret what happened *and* I want us to start feeling happier together.

(That's a good insight. Couples tend to focus on one extreme or the other—focusing only on the past or only on the future—and that's not the most helpful.)

LINDA: Sometimes what helps me is when I'm watching you and you don't know I'm watching. If I like what I see I feel better about you. But when I see you being lazy around the house or impatient with the kids, it annoys me.

FRANK: But I don't want to always act like I'm under scrutiny. It's normal for a parent to get impatient with children or not to feel like doing housework.

LINDA: I know. I'm not saying you're wrong. I'm saying it's easier to warm up to you and appreciate you when I see you being helpful or considerate.

FRANK: It's like dating someone for the first time. Everything I do is analyzed.

LINDA: Right. And in a way we are starting out all over again. I don't know you as well as I thought I did. But I'm trying to give you the benefit of the doubt.

(Being able to give the benefit of the doubt marks an important shift. It's a good sign.)

FRANK: Will our lives ever be normal again?

LINDA: Let's just try to make things better week by week.

As devastating as affairs can be, they are overcome every day by couples devoted to making their marriage work. These are some of the most difficult conversations spouses may ever have. A willingness to persist over many months and not make rash judgments about the future of the marriage is necessary—along with regular conversations and a plan of action to rebuild the relationship.

"We need to talk"

Chapter Fourteen

Ten Quick Conversations

By now you've probably read a number of chapters and have started developing a feel for how to have an effective conversation. While the particular topics might vary, there is an underlying structure to most effective conversations that is similar from one topic to the next, best exemplified by the SAIL approach in Chapter 2. One way to learn is to read transcripts of effective conversations, like the ones in this book. It doesn't matter if the particular topic is relevant to your marriage. Your goal is to get a feel for how a successful conversation looks.

This chapter will present a hodgepodge of topics where couples might get stuck. In this chapter you will find brief examples, without frills, of how those conversations can proceed with maximum effectiveness. Imagine that the tone of these conversations is at least moderately respectful. Gentle openings are essential. No conversation will be successful if it contains harsh tones or an attacking style.

YOU: Sweetheart, I get frustrated when you ask me for things while I'm working from home. I'm frustrated because I don't wish to push you away but at the same time I really need to not be interrupted. **(Defining the problem.)**

SPOUSE: Fine, fine, I'll leave you alone. *(A defensive response.)*

YOU: It's not just that. I really want you to understand my viewpoint and not be pissed at me when I don't want to be disturbed. I'm just asking you to be aware that I have work to do and it isn't easy to simply stop what I'm doing. **(Clarifying the problem and making a polite request.)**

SPOUSE: It's confusing because when I do leave you alone you sometimes seek me out or take a break so I'm left with the impression that you're not that busy.

YOU: You're right, I do that sometimes and I can see why you think I'm not busy. **(Validating the spouse.)**

SPOUSE: And sometimes I'm not really intruding. I'm just asking if I can get you something.

YOU: And I appreciate that. Maybe what I'm really saying is that when you interrupt me and I say "not now," I don't want you to get mad. Just understand that unless there's an emergency, my work has to come first. Can you do that?

SPOUSE: Okay. But can I get your attention when you take a break? Or would you rather I act as if you're at work and not disturb you?

YOU: Sometimes when I take a break I'm still thinking. I'm just getting up and stretching but I still feel like I'm focusing on my work.

SPOUSE: So what should I do?

YOU: No need to walk on eggshells. Talk to me and ask questions but be understanding and tolerant if I say this isn't the right time.

SPOUSE: Okay.

SCENARIO: Your spouse swears too much. It especially bothers you in some social situations, but even when it's just the two of you his use of the "F" word rankles.

YOU: It bothers me a lot when you swear. I've asked you not to and you say you will stop but it seems to me there hasn't been much improvement.

SPOUSE: You seem to be the only person who gets upset about it.

YOU: I'm sure some don't. I'm not asking for a debate on whether or not swearing is socially acceptable. I'm asking you to do me a favor and please not swear, at least when I'm around. **(This was a useful response. It avoided a senseless debate.)**

SPOUSE: All right, all right.

YOU: I appreciate that. But I wonder if you'll resent me for this or if something else I'm doing is bothering you.

SPOUSE: Sometimes I think you make mountains out of molehills. Not just about swearing, but a number of things. I feel like if I don't do things the way you want I pay a price.

YOU: The next time I do that, please bring it to my attention. I don't want you to think I'm that controlling. But I still wish you wouldn't swear.

SPOUSE: Okay, I'll try harder not to swear around you. But I'd like you to take me seriously when I point out situations where I think you're too demanding.

YOU: It's a deal.

SCENARIO: Your spouse "teases" you, sometimes in public. You find it upsetting. Your spouse thinks you're just too sensitive.

YOU: I really don't like being the butt of your jokes. I know you think I don't have a sense of humor and that you mean nothing by your teasing, but I'm asking you not to do it.

SPOUSE: It's innocent fun.

YOU: Sweetheart, that's not my point. I'm not discussing whether it's innocent or not. I'm making a very strong request. Please do not tease me in public. I don't like it. **(It's a good idea not to accuse the spouse of bad intentions. It will lead to a debate.)**

SPOUSE: Okay, but I wish you'd lighten up.

YOU: You want to make this a problem about me. I'm not accusing you of being purposely hurtful. I'm not making it about you. I'm saying that as your wife I do not wish to be teased or innocently made fun of in public. Are you willing to do that for me?

SPOUSE: Okay.

YOU: Thank you. But I'm holding you to your promise. This is really very important to me.

SCENARIO: Your spouse expects you to do most of the talking, inviting, entertaining, and greeting-card writing when it comes to his side of the family. You want him to take on more of the responsibility.

YOU: This time I'd like you to send out Christmas cards to your side of the family. And I'd like you to talk with your mother more when she calls—not simply give the phone to me.

SPOUSE: What's the matter, don't you like my family?

YOU: Yes I do. But too much of the responsibility is on my plate. It's my fault, too. Over the years I've gone along with it this way.

SPOUSE: But you're a better conversationalist.

YOU: That may be. But what I'm saying is that I don't intend to do as much of the work as I once did when it comes to entertaining your family. I love them and I'll be sociable. But you'll have to get more involved because I'm getting less involved. **(This is an important shift. It is no longer telling him what to do but rather you are telling him what _you_ intend to do.)**

SPOUSE: Why the sudden change?

YOU: I'm not mad at you or them. I'm just tired. If you want your family to receive Christmas cards please go out and buy them and send them out. And when your mom calls I'll certainly speak to her but I'm passing the phone to you, as well.

SPOUSE: What if my family thinks you're mad at them?

YOU: I'll always be friendly. If they ask me about it I'll explain my reasons and I'm sure they'll understand.

SCENARIO: You like a little more cuddling or affection. Your spouse says "I wasn't raised that way."

YOU: I know we've discussed this before but we've never come to a satisfying solution. I want you to show me more affection even though it's awkward for you.

SPOUSE: I feel like I'm doing something by force. I don't like that feeling.

YOU: That's one way of looking at it. Another way is to simply go out of your way a little bit more for me because I'm your wife. It's just as awkward for me to have to settle for less affection—but I do that for you.

SPOUSE: I never thought of it like that. But I also wish you could just accept me as I am.

YOU: And if you accept me as *I* am, you'll need to put up with the fact that I need more affection. Acceptance goes both ways.

SPOUSE: So how do we go about this?

YOU: We can be creative. But I think if you simply tried to show more affection every day, I'd be happier and you might find that over time you'll be less self-conscious.

SPOUSE: What if I forget?

YOU: This is important to me so I'll remind you.

SCENARIO: Scenario: Your spouse shows favoritism to one child.

YOU: I'd like to point something out that's important. I noticed that when Billy forgets to do something you cut him slack, but when Jackie forgets you give her a hard time.

SPOUSE: I don't think that's true.

YOU: It's possible I'm misreading this but I'd like you to think that it's possible you are favoring one child over another.

SPOUSE: But I'm not.

YOU: I'm asking you to consider the possibility. You may not be doing it on purpose.

SPOUSE: Jackie is more defiant. If I'm harder on her, maybe that's why.

YOU: That's also possible. I'm not saying you're wrong or a bad parent. I'm asking you to pay more attention to how you react to each of our children. I really think you can be much harder on Jackie.

SPOUSE: Well, I don't think it's as bad as you think.

YOU: That might be. If it's okay with you, I'll point it out when I see it happening. Is that all right?

SPOUSE: Okay.

YOU: And I'm sure you'll say you have a reason when I do point it out. I'm not asking you to justify your actions, I'm asking you to be open to the idea that you may be tougher on one of the kids.

SCENARIO: You'd like more emotional space just as a way to relax and clear your head. Your spouse feels a bit rejected by that and also views it as your way to get out of home responsibilities.

SPOUSE: Just what do you mean by needing space?

YOU: I just feel I have practically no time to myself. Even if I'm not busy I feel like I'm "on call" with the kids and even with you.

SPOUSE: You don't like spending time with me?

YOU: I put a lot of pressure on myself to make myself available and I feel guilty when I pull away.

SPOUSE: I don't feel a need to have so much time away from you.

YOU: This isn't about wanting to be away from you. It's about wanting more time for me. I need some kind of regular outlet. Maybe just an occasional half-day off where I can do what I want.

SPOUSE: That sounds fine in theory, but if you take a day off it means everything's left for me to do.

YOU: I know. And that isn't easy. But you can have some time for yourself, too. I'd be happy to give you that.

SPOUSE: But I don't need that.

YOU: If I have more free time and you have to pick up the slack, you may discover you do need more time for yourself.

SPOUSE: I guess.

YOU: You sound a little hurt or worried. I'm really just asking for a few more breaks from the action; something to recharge my batteries. It doesn't have to be a regular thing. We can take it week to week and work around what needs to happen here. I just want to know that I can take some extra time for myself here or there and not feel like I have to explain myself or get permission every time.

SCENARIO: Your spouse is a sports fanatic. Whenever his team loses he is in a miserable mood for hours.

YOU: It wasn't a good day for you or your team. But do you want to hear about my day? I had to listen to my husband scream at the TV while he ignored his wife and children. Then I had to put up with him sulking the rest of the day.

SPOUSE: You're exaggerating.

YOU: If it happened only occasionally I'd put up with it. But it happens a couple of times a week. It really has become a problem for me. I get turned off from you for days afterward.

SPOUSE: You know I love baseball.

YOU: It's important that you hear what I'm trying to say. Of course I know you love baseball. But when your team is losing no one can come near you. You're a grizzly bear. You take out your frustrations on me and the kids. It has to stop.

SPOUSE: The kids don't take it personally, why should you?

YOU: I can see that we disagree about the effect you're having. You don't have to agree with me. But I'm asking you to tone it down and be friendlier to your family when your team is losing.

SPOUSE: I don't think I'm that bad.

YOU: You keep wanting to make this a debate. I'm saying that no matter how well behaved you think you are, it's upsetting to me.

Next time it happens I will point it out. And I simply want you to pull back and be less agitated when I point it out. Don't challenge me about it, just ease off. Are you willing to do that?

SCENARIO: Your spouse insists on saving money by constantly switching off lights that were left on, turning off the air conditioning when you're sweltering, and lecturing about how often you waste energy.

YOU: I know how you feel about the cost of electricity but I don't agree with you about how far we should go to save money. You're frustrated with me and I'm frustrated with you.

SPOUSE: I think you waste energy.

YOU: But this is our problem: Sure, we can save even more money by cutting back on energy usage. I agree with you on that. But you cut back to a level I don't want to live by, and then you get agitated and lecture me.

SPOUSE: Because I don't think you take my concerns seriously.

YOU: Actually, I do. There are many times I'm inconvenienced but I put up with it because it's what you want. I'm asking that you do the same for me.

SPOUSE: I do! I see lights left on all the time and I never say a word.

YOU: Thank you. So it seems each of us is already compromising but the problem is we don't realize just how much we're already doing for one another.

SPOUSE: Maybe that's true.

YOU: There isn't an easy answer to this problem. We both won't be fully satisfied all the time. I need to be as mindful as I can be about energy usage, and I'd like you to ease up on turning off lights or lecturing me about what the thermostat should be set at. **(This is a perpetual problem that can only be managed, not solved.)**

SPOUSE: Why can't I turn off a light that's been left on?

YOU: You can. But I'm asking you to not be so quick. Sometimes I just leave a room for a minute and when I return the light is off. And if I do forget, don't make a big deal out of it. And I won't make a big deal out of it when I sometimes think you're overdoing it. We just have to make the best of it because we'll never agree.

SCENARIO: If you complain to your spouse about something long after it happened, your spouse says "Why didn't you tell me about it before now?" But if you bring up complaints right away, your spouse gets defensive or dismissive.

YOU: I feel like I'm in a no-win situation. I'm wrong for bringing things up right away or I'm wrong for waiting to bring them up.

SPOUSE: Just because you have a complaint doesn't mean I have to agree with you. And if I disagree, that doesn't mean I'm being difficult. I'm just telling you how I see things.

YOU: I think the problem is that if you don't agree with me you don't see the purpose of continuing the conversation.

SPOUSE: Why should we continue to debate?

YOU: I don't think we should debate at all. We get stuck in right versus wrong. It isn't always about that. It's about being friends. Sometimes when you're friends you go along with something you don't want or you look for the grain of truth in something your friend says instead of pointing out what you don't agree with.

SPOUSE: I don't understand.

YOU: If I have a complaint, it means I want something to be different. We never discuss what can be different because we're debating whether or not my complaint is valid.

SPOUSE: But if your complaint isn't valid, why should I change?

YOU: What I'd like to see happen is for you to take my concerns seriously—even if you don't agree completely with my assessment. And I will take your views seriously. Then we need to come up with a plan that takes into consideration both of our views. I want us to cooperate more with each other.

Staying on Track

As you can see, patience is a good quality to have when trying to improve dialogues. Even the best communicators will have bad days or will struggle with certain topics. Effective communicators are like professional athletes or entertainers—they have to keep practicing and stay in shape. It's not hard to veer off track.

Good communication does wonders for your relationship and helps to build goodwill. With enough goodwill you can afford to make communication mistakes without paying a penalty. By rereading sections of this book from time to time, you may discover that staying on track is not so complicated.

Appendix

A Sample Script
for Quick Reference

Manipulation and Game-Playing, see page 40 for full script

"We need to talk"

TONI: You didn't kiss me goodbye this morning.

PHIL: I forgot.

TONI: You forget a lot of things. Remember I asked you to repair the light switch in the hallway? It's been weeks.

PHIL: It's not like I've been watching TV all this time.

TONI: It's just that I feel you do what you want and don't really pay attention to me.

This is getting off to a rough start. If she tries to pick apart everything that bothers her, Phil will feel attacked. Better to open with something less accusatory and get to the heart of the matter quickly.

TONI: Let me start over. I don't want to sound so critical. I've noticed that when I think you're being uncooperative, I try to get even in small ways. Maybe you've seen me moping around and acting unhappy.

PHIL: Yes.

TONI: I'm hoping you can admit that you do similar things to me.

PHIL: I stay out of your way. That's what I do.

TONI: Like when you didn't kiss me goodbye this morning.

PHIL: I guess I do it to annoy you and avoid an argument.

TONI: Thank you for admitting that. Another thing I've noticed is that when I have to ask you repeatedly to do something for me, you try to make me feel guilty when you're the one who's made promises he didn't keep.

PHIL: Not always.

TONI: True. But I'd really appreciate it if you would go with the spirit of this conversation. I'm saying we each do things to displease the other when we're angry and not able to talk about what's bothering us.

This is a good example of trying to stay on track. The point is not to debate facts about certain events but to recognize that they each can be manipulative.

PHIL: When I complain to you, I think you get defensive, like I'm not supposed to feel the way I do. That's why I'd rather not talk.

TONI: Like when you're annoyed that I don't feel like having sex?

PHIL: Right. Good example. You make me feel I'm wrong to want it.

This is a good place for Toni to say to herself, "I accept my spouse is blaming me right now and not looking at his contribution to the problem." Acceptance will tone down her annoyance.

TONI: You're right. I have done that and I shouldn't. But I do it because it's connected to how I think you treat me overall. You make me feel I'm wrong to want you to fix a light switch. I try to be patient, give you all the time you want. Then you don't follow up and

I'm the bad guy for complaining. I think we each make each other feel guilty.

PHIL: I see that.

TONI: Aren't you tired of being aggravated with me so much?

PHIL: Yeah. What can we do to fix it?

Good. The conversation is getting to the "what to do" part. That happens more quickly and effortlessly when there are no stubborn debates and each side is willing to admit mistakes.

TONI: Somehow we have to be willing to speak up more rather than communicate indirectly.

PHIL: But what if I speak up and still don't get what I want?

TONI: But what if you do? And what if I don't get what I want? We have to be willing to stop looking at a conversation as having a winner and a loser. Sometimes we get our way, sometimes we don't, and sometimes we compromise.

PHIL: Let's give it a try and see what happens.

Index

Abusiveness
  lying and, 33
  scenario illustrating, 31, 32
  signs of control and, 33–34
Acceptance, 25–26, 50
Adversity, 57–71
  coping with situation vs. coping with
    feelings, 58–59
  dialogue do's, 62–65
  fears of expressing feelings and, 61–62,
    63
  female default response, 60
  follow-through phase, 68
  male default response, 59–60
  marriage (emotional) immune system
    and, 57–60
  openings for discussing, 65–67
  sample script, 69–71
Affairs. *See* Cheating
Anxiety. *See also specific topics*
  anger, guilt, depression and, 23
  eyes revealing, 4–5
  fear of further upset and, 61
  follow-throughs and, 38–42, 134–38
  intensifying conversations, 2–4
  managing, 4, 22–23, 38–42, 61,
    134–38
  reprogramming brain and, 35–36
  sensitivity and, 3–4
Apathy. *See* Emotional distance
Arguments, escalating/de-escalating, 14–16
Attitudes, persisting, 18–19
Awareness, of problems, 12–13

Black-and-white mentality, 9–11
Body language, 4–6
Book overview, ix–x

Cheating, 181–94
  depressed-accepting phase, 185,
    189–90
  follow-throughs, 186–91
  immediate consequences of, 183–84
  openings for discussing, 186–91
  phases of repair, 184–91
  reasons for, 182–83
  rebirth phase, 185–86, 190–91
  roller coaster phase, 185, 186–89
  sample script, 191–94
  statistics and tendencies, 181–82
Childhood
  do-it-yourself child, 96
  emotional gaps in, 21–22
  interfering with parenting skills, 94–96
  overfunctioning child, 95–96
  questions about growing up, 21–23
  underfunctioning child, 95
Chores. *See* Money and chores
"Clash, Rehash, and Dash" pattern, 1–2, 64
Complaints, brining up, 204–5
Connectedness. *See* Emotional distance
Conversational traps
  allowing arguments to escalate, 14–16
  anxiety as basis of, 2–4
  black-and-white mentality, 9–11
  "Clash, Rehash, and Dash" pattern, 1–2
  confusing feelings with facts, 13–14
  five toxic traps, 7–16
  rough start-ups, 8–9
  that all problems can be solved, 11–13
  what senses can tell you, 4–6

Do-it-yourself child, 96
Dreams. *See* Unfulfilled dreams

Index